JAMESTOWN  EDUCATION

W9-AZC-637

In the Spotlight™

Volume 1

Levels
H–J

Henry Billings
Melissa Billings

 Glencoe

New York, New York   Columbus, Ohio   Chicago, Illinois   Peoria, Illinois   Woodland Hills, California

JAMESTOWN EDUCATION

The McGraw·Hill Companies

Copyright © 2007 The McGraw-Hill Companies, Inc.
All rights reserved. Except as permitted under the United States
Copyright Act, no part of this publication may be reproduced or
distributed in any form or by any means, or stored in a database or
retrieval system, without prior written permission of the publisher.

ISBN-13: 978-0-07-874321-4
ISBN-10: 0-07-874321-4

Send all queries to:
Glencoe/McGraw-Hill
8787 Orion Place
Columbus, OH 43240-4027

2 3 4 5 6 7 8 9 10 021 10 09 08 07

Contents

Unit Three

To the Student

This book has nine articles about celebrities, or famous people, in the world today. Some of the celebrities are movie or television stars. Some are sports players. Others are authors or musicians.

The lives of these stars can inspire us. Some of the stars had tough times while growing up. They worked very hard to find success. Others had to stay focused on their dreams even when other people thought they would fail. And some had to get through challenges even after they became well-known.

In this book you will work on these three specific reading skills:

Asking Questions to Get Information

Fact and Opinion

Drawing Conclusions

You will also work on other reading and vocabulary skills. This will help you understand and think about what you read. The lessons include types of questions often found on state and national tests. Completing the questions can help you get ready for tests you may have to take later.

How to Use This Book

About the Book

This book has three units. Each unit has three lessons. Each lesson has an article about a celebrity followed by practice exercises.

Working Through Each Lesson

Photo Start each lesson by looking at the photo. Read the title and subtitle to get an idea of what the article will focus on.

Think About What You Know, Word Power, Reading Skill This page will help you prepare to read.

Article Now read about the celebrity. Enjoy!

Activities Complete all the activities. Then check your work. Your teacher will give you an answer key to do this. Record the number of your correct answers for each activity. At the end of the lesson, add up your total score for parts A, B, and C. Then find your percentage score in the table. Record your percentage score on the Comprehension and Critical Thinking Progress Graph on page 105.

Compare and Contrast Chart At the end of each unit, you will complete a Compare and Contrast Chart. The chart will help you see what some of the celebrities in the unit have in common.

My Personal Dictionary In the back of this book, you can jot down words you would like to know more about. Later you can ask your teacher or a classmate what the words mean. Then you can add the definitions in your own words.

Serena Williams

Coldplay

Lisa Fernandez

Serena Williams

More Than Just a Tennis Star

Birth Name Serena Williams

Birth Date and Place September 26, 1981; Saginaw, Michigan

Homes Los Angeles, California, and Palm Beach Gardens, Florida

Think About What You Know

What do you think is most important in life? What are your priorities? Read the article to find out how Serena Williams balances her tennis career with the other priorities in her life.

Word Power

What do the words below tell you about the article?

perfectionist someone who sets extremely high personal standards

insatiable not able to be satisfied

sharecropper a farmer who farms on someone else's land in return for a share of the crops

illiterates people who are unable to read or write

endorsing giving support or approval to

Reading Skill

Asking Questions to Get Information Good readers **ask questions.** Asking and answering questions as you read can help you find the most important ideas in the text. Make sure to ask questions about the big ideas. Asking questions that start with *what, where, when, how,* and *why* can help you find the big ideas.

Example

Homeschooling offers an alternative to traditional education. Homeschooled children don't go to a school building. They are taught by a parent or teacher at home. Parents choose to homeschool their children for many different reasons. They may be unhappy with the quality of the local schools, or a family may decide to homeschool for religious reasons.

"*Why* do parents choose to homeschool their children?" is one good question you might ask yourself to find important information. What is another question you might ask to find important information?

Serena Williams

More Than Just a Tennis Star

If you had devoted your entire childhood to tennis and then had battled your way through tournament after tournament to become one of the very best players in the world, tennis would likely be the most important thing in your life, right? Well, maybe not—at least not if your name is Serena Williams.

2   When Williams made her first appearance on the world tennis scene in the late 1990s, she impressed everyone with her athletic ability. She and her sister Venus, who is 15 months older, seemed destined to lead the way in women's tennis for years to come. Although Williams was just a teenager, she displayed enormous confidence and commitment to her sport, telling reporters, "I fear no one" and "I know what I want. I want not to lose a match."

3   Williams's dedication to tennis was obvious. "When I am on the court, it is kind of like my life depends on it," she said. She also declared, "I'm a **perfectionist.** I'm pretty much **insatiable.** I feel there's so much I can improve on." But while tennis was clearly one of her top priorities, it wasn't first on the list. For her, family, religion, and education have always been more important. To understand why, it helps to remember Williams's background.

4   Williams grew up in Compton, California, a section of Los Angeles challenged by high crime and poverty. Her father, Richard, was the son of a Louisiana **sharecropper,** and her mother, Oracene, was a nurse from Mississippi. Richard believed that tennis could help his daughters escape a life of poverty, so when they were very young he began teaching them to play. The three older sisters didn't show particular talent with a racket, but the two youngest—Venus and Serena—did.

5   For six hours every day Richard worked with his daughters, looking up information from a tennis manual and shouting it out to them as they bounded around the court. Playing at Compton's public

facilities, the girls learned to ignore the gangs that were always hanging around and the occasional sound of gunfire and police sirens. They learned to focus solely on the ball.

6   Serena competed in her first tournament when she was just four and a half, and by the time she was ten, both she and Venus were playing on the national junior tennis circuit, the place where most promising players sharpen their skills before turning pro. Richard, however, didn't like having his children in such a competitive environment. He also thought the tennis world was "lily-white" and worried that his daughters would encounter racism. He therefore took them off the circuit, moved the family to Florida, and continued working with them on his own.

7   Consequently, Serena Williams didn't spend much time with other young tennis players except, of course, for her sister Venus. She didn't spend much time with classmates, either, because starting at age 12 she was homeschooled by her mother. This schooling was something the whole family took seriously. "My girls are very great players," Richard declared, "and they'll win lots of tournaments, but I'll tell you what I tell them: education is much more important." He bluntly told one reporter, "When they've finished their tennis careers, I don't want a couple of gum-chewing **illiterates** on my hands."

Skill Break
Asking Questions to Get Information
Look at paragraph 6 on this page. The paragraph describes what happened after Williams competed in her first tournament.

What would be a good **question** to ask to find the **important information** in this paragraph?

What is the **answer** to your question?

8   And so for Serena and Venus Williams, life consisted of family, schoolwork, religion, and tennis. The family had its share of troubles—in fact, Richard and Oracene divorced in 2002—but Serena felt an intense bond with all the members of her family. "Family's first," she said, "and that's what matters most." To her, "tennis is just a game, family is forever."

9   Williams maintained this attitude as she made her quick ascent up through the ranks of professional tennis. At age 16, when she was ranked 304th in the world, she stunned tennis fans by beating 7th-ranked Mary Pierce. By age 18, she had moved into the top ten. And at age 21, Williams became the number-one female tennis player in the world, taking the title away from her sister Venus.

10   Without a doubt, Williams was at the top of her game. Opponents and observers alike expressed awe at her speed and the power of her serves, which often came blasting over the net at 120 miles per hour.

11   Williams relished the praise, yet she knew that athletic success was a fleeting thing. When asked what advice she liked to give young fans, she said, "I like to stress the importance of education, especially in sports, because you never know what could happen." While growing her tennis career, Williams made sure to nurture her other interests, particularly acting. She began doing guest spots on TV shows and investigated the possibility of starring in a Hollywood film.

12   Williams's balanced perspective about her sport proved useful in the summer of 2003, when she injured her knee in a tournament and needed surgery to repair it. But before her knee had fully healed, something much worse happened. In September 2003, Serena's oldest sister, Yetunde, was shot and killed while she sat in her car. Serena,

Fun Facts

- Serena Williams enjoys surfing and playing guitar.
- She has studied fashion design at the Art Institute of Florida.
- She and her sister Venus appeared in their own reality TV show in 2005.
- Her favorite place to visit is Italy.

Serena (right) and Venus Williams pose together after winning the women's doubles championship in the 2001 Australian Open.

Venus, and the entire Williams family were devastated, and Serena didn't return to competition until early in 2004.

13   Being out of competition for so long made it difficult for her to remain in peak condition, so when she did return she struggled to win her matches and was troubled by various injuries. People wondered if her best days of tennis were behind her. Williams insisted they weren't, saying, "As long as I'm healthy I'm still definitely a top competitor."

14   In 2005 Williams proved that she was still one of the world's best players by capturing the Australian Open singles championship. At the same time, though, she knew that it didn't really matter if she continued to win or not. She had already secured a prominent place in the history of women's tennis. And she had already earned enough money to last for the rest of her life. She had made $13 million playing in tournaments and another $60 million by **endorsing** products. Besides, Yetunde's death had underscored her long-standing belief that "there is more out there than winning and losing the tournament."

15   Even as she continues to work on her tennis career, she keeps her eye out for acting roles and has begun experimenting with fashion design. Despite her phenomenal talent as a tennis player, Serena Williams clearly isn't kidding when she says, "I've never considered tennis as my only outlet."

A Understanding What You Read

◆ Fill in the circle next to the correct answer or write the answer.

1. Unlike Venus and Serena, the three oldest Williams sisters
   - ○ A. did not go to church every Sunday.
   - ○ B. were not homeschooled by their mother.
   - ○ C. did not show any talent for tennis.

2. Choose from the letters below to correctly complete the following statement. Write the letters on the lines.

   On the negative side, _____, but on the positive side, _____.

   A. Venus and Serena learned to focus solely on the ball

   B. Venus and Serena stopped playing on the national junior circuit

   C. Venus and Serena had to practice around gangs and gunfire

3. In which paragraph did you find the information to answer question 2?

   _____

4. Which of the following statements is an opinion rather than a fact?
   - ○ A. Williams's dedication to tennis was obvious.
   - ○ B. Williams began doing guest spots on TV shows.
   - ○ C. Williams became the top female tennis player in the world.

5. In addition to tennis, Williams is also interested in
   - ○ A. working on crime prevention.
   - ○ B. acting in Hollywood movies.
   - ○ C. being a sports announcer.

_____ Number of Correct Answers: Part A

B Asking Questions to Get Information

◆ Read the paragraph below. Fill in the circle next to the **best** question to ask to find important information in the paragraph.

1.

Consequently, Serena Williams didn't spend much time with other young tennis players except, of course, for her sister Venus. She didn't spend much time with classmates, either, because starting at age 12 she was homeschooled by her mother. This schooling was something the whole family took seriously. "My girls are very great players," Richard declared, "and they'll win lots of tournaments, but I'll tell you what I tell them: education is much more important." He bluntly told one reporter, "When they've finished their tennis careers, I don't want a couple of gum-chewing illiterates on my hands."

○ A. When did Serena's mother start homeschooling her?
○ B. What does the Williams family think about education?
○ C. Why was Richard Williams talking to reporters?

◆ Reread paragraph 12 in the article. Write **one** question that would help you find the most important information in the paragraph. Then write the answer to your question.

2. Question: _____

_____

Answer: _____

_____

_____ Number of Correct Answers: Part B

C Using Words

◆ Cross out one of the four words in each row that does not relate to the word in dark type.

1. perfectionist

expectation   quality   collection   error

2. insatiable

playful   eager   thirsty   wanting

3. sharecropper

occupation   acre   harvest   distance

4. illiterates

newspaper   pledge   tutor   weakness

5. endorsing

advertisement   promotion   communication   nutrition

◆ Choose one of the words shown in dark type above. Write a sentence using the word.

6. word: _____

_____

_____

_____ Number of Correct Answers: Part C

10

D Writing About It

Write a Speech

◆ Suppose you were going to give a speech about Serena Williams. Write a speech about Williams's life, her family, and her tennis career. Write **at least four** sentences. Use the checklist on page 103 to check your work.

_____

_____

_____

_____

_____

_____

_____

_____

Lesson 1 Add your correct answers from parts A, B, and C to get your total score. Then find the percentage for your total score on the chart below. Record your percentage on the graph on page 105.

_____ Total Score for Parts A, B, and C

_____ Percentage

Total Score	1	2	3	4	5	6	7	8	9	10	11	12	13
Percentage	8	15	23	31	38	46	54	62	69	77	85	92	100

Coldplay
True to Themselves

Band Members' Names Chris Martin, Guy Berryman, Jonny Buckland, Will Champion

Date and Place Founded January 8, 1998; London, England

Band Members' Homes England and North Wales

Think About What You Know

Do you like to listen to popular music? What are your favorite bands? Read the article to find out about the rock band Coldplay, its music, and its fans.

Word Power

What do the words below tell you about the article?

effusive showing excessive feelings

insufferable unbearable or not to be tolerated

banter good-natured, witty conversation

integrity honesty or moral decency

accolades praise, awards, or honors

Reading Skill

Fact and Opinion A **fact** is a statement that can be proved by checking a reference source. An **opinion** is someone's own idea or belief about something. When a statement includes words that show judgment, such as *best* or *should,* that statement usually contains someone's opinion. Nouns and adjectives that show judgment, such as *excellent* or *masterpiece,* may also indicate that a statement is an opinion.

Example

Fact   The Beatles released their first album in 1963. Their bright melodies and playful personalities won fans all

Opinion   over the world. Their recordings were the most significant musical accomplishment of the twentieth century.

The statement "The Beatles released their first album in 1963" is a fact that can be proved. The statement "Their recordings were the most significant musical accomplishment of the twentieth century" shows a judgment about music in the twentieth century. It is an opinion. What phrase in the second statement shows that it is an opinion?

Coldplay

True to Themselves

Coldplay is hot. It's one of the hottest bands around, and has been since it emerged in 2000 with its debut album, *Parachutes.* Its second effort, *A Rush of Blood to the Head,* increased the band's musical stature, and its third album, *X & Y,* cemented its reputation as one of the most accomplished bands to come along in years. The praise for Coldplay has been so **effusive** that even Chris Martin, the group's lead singer, has been taken aback, saying, "The more successful we become, the stranger it gets."

2   What exactly are people saying about Coldplay? *Entertainment Weekly* has praised the group's "quiet, intense intelligence." *Rolling Stone* has called their music "sparse, emotional soundscapes that drip with melancholy and hit you squarely in the gut." And the *All Music Guide* has labeled Coldplay's work "fresh," "passionate," and "heart-rending." Music fans, meanwhile, have spoken with their wallets, buying the band's albums and downloading singles from the Internet in staggering numbers.

3   But not everyone adores Coldplay. Record executive Alan McGee has made very unfavorable comments about the band's music and *New York Times* music critic Jon Pareles refers to Coldplay as "the most **insufferable** band of the decade." These views, however, are in the minority. In fact, according to Dave Tallis of the British Broadcasting Corporation, whose opinion may be more reflective of popular opinion, their third album is an undeniable masterpiece. He writes, "This album is superb. It'll silence their critics, amaze their fans, and win them a whole new legion of admirers. It might even bring about world peace!"

4   Behind all the **banter** and hype about the band stand four musicians: Chris Martin doing lead vocals and piano, Jonny Buckland at lead guitar, Guy Berryman playing bass, and Will Champion

on drums. Martin has the broadest name recognition, not only because he's the lead singer but also because of his 2003 marriage to Hollywood star Gwyneth Paltrow. Yet each band member has enormous talent and each has made vital contributions to the band. "We all have quite different musical backgrounds . . . we all bring our individuality into the band and the music," says Berryman.

5   Coldplay formed back in the mid 1990s, when these four men were college students in London, England. Martin and Buckland met the very first week of school and were immediately drawn together by their love of music. They spent much of freshman year composing songs and planning a band.

6   Martin had grown up in Devon, England, playing the piano for his schoolteacher mother and accountant father. In boarding school he mastered the guitar and spent hours listening to the thoughtful lyrics of Tom Waits, Bob Dylan, and Neil Young. His beautiful voice made him a natural lead singer.

7   Buckland had grown up in North Wales with a father who loved the heavy guitar work of Jimi Hendrix and an older brother who loved an Irish rock band called My Bloody Valentine. Immersed in those sounds, Buckland began playing the guitar when he was eleven. He was the perfect man to play lead guitar.

8   Another freshman in Martin and Buckland's residence hall was Guy Berryman. The Scottish-born Berryman had grown up listening to funk music and loved its emphasis on a heavy bass line, so he was a logical choice to play bass.

Skill Break
Fact and Opinion
Look at paragraph 7 on this page. The paragraph describes the musical beginnings of Coldplay's Jonny Buckland.

Which statement in this paragraph shows someone's **opinion?**

What **clue words** did you use?

9   That left drums, which Will Champion from Southampton, England, was eager to handle. Champion played many instruments, from guitar to bass to piano to tin whistle. He had no experience with percussion instruments but wanted to be part of this extraordinary group, and he picked up drums without too much trouble.

10   With the players in place, the group began generating songs, spending hours each week writing and practicing new pieces. According to Martin, "we used to play in bathrooms, the basement, even in the park—anywhere we could find to play."

11   They had no idea what the future held for them, but they had hopes of achieving great success. "We were determined to do it, from the start," says Buckland, "and from the moment I met Chris I really did think that we could go all the way."

12   Underlying their hopes was a belief that the music they were creating was exceptionally good. "As soon as we played together," says Champion, "it was much better than anything else we'd ever heard."

13   By 1998 they were ready to play for a public audience. Coldplay began performing in small clubs and got together enough money to make a record, giving out most of the 500 copies to friends and record companies. That led to a contract with the Fierce Panda record label and eventually a five-album contract with Parlophone Records in 1999. By then Berryman had decided he didn't want to pursue an engineering degree, so he dropped out of college. The other three band members, however, completed their studies. It was only when they graduated that they were free to devote their lives to music.

Fun Facts

- Coldplay donates 10 percent of their earnings to charity.
- The band's original name was Starfish.
- They have turned down advertising offers worth millions of dollars because they refuse to sell their songs for use in commercials.

Chris Martin performs with Coldplay at a music and arts festival in California.

14   By the time Coldplay's first album was finished, Martin and the others had set some ground rules to protect the group's **integrity** and prevent discord. First of all, they agreed that all profits would be shared equally among the four members. Secondly, as Berryman puts it, "we all have equal say. It takes only one person to disagree with something for it to be vetoed." Finally, the members agreed that they had a responsibility both to their fans and to each other to be clear-headed about their music, so they made strict rules against drug use.

15   With these rules in place, the band went on to achieve super-stardom, with some people comparing Coldplay to U2 or even the Beatles. Despite the pressure caused by this kind of comparison, Coldplay has continued to follow its own path. The release of Coldplay's second album was delayed because the band members weren't satisfied with it and wanted to rework many of the songs. They did the same thing with their third album. As Martin told one reporter, "We're trying to get to the very highest level. We want to be better than *Mozart*. That doesn't mean we are, but that's what we're trying for."

16   Certainly everyone in the band hopes the public will continue to appreciate their work, but more than that, they feel the need to be true to their own artistic and musical visions. As Champion says, despite all the **accolades** that Coldplay has received, they are still "just four friends trying to make great music."

A Understanding What You Read

◆ Fill in the circle next to the correct answer.

1. The author probably wrote this article in order to

  ○ A. encourage the reader to see Coldplay perform live.

  ○ B. inform the reader about Coldplay's music and success.

  ○ C. express an opinion about Coldplay's band members.

2. Growing up, the members of Coldplay were influenced by

  ○ A. Bob Dylan, Jimi Hendrix, and funk music.

  ○ B. The Rolling Stones, David Bowie, and rap music.

  ○ C. The Beatles, Pink Floyd, and blues music.

3. Coldplay signed a contract with Fierce Panda Records after

  ○ A. all the band's members finished college.

  ○ B. the band made 500 copies of a record.

  ○ C. the band canceled its deal with Parlophone.

4. What are the **two** causes of Chris Martin's broad name recognition?

  ○ A. He grew up in Devon and went to boarding school.

  ○ B. He is the lead singer and he is married to a movie star.

  ○ C. He has a beautiful voice and he plays the guitar.

5. From the information in the article, you can predict that Coldplay will

  ○ A. record songs written by Mozart.

  ○ B. make a new album as quickly as possible.

  ○ C. maintain their rule against using drugs.

_____ Number of Correct Answers: Part A

B Understanding Fact and Opinion

◆ Read the paragraph below. Write the letter *O* on the lines next to the statements that show someone's opinion. Write the letter *F* on the lines next to the statements that are facts.

1.

But not everyone adores Coldplay. Record executive Alan McGee has made very unfavorable comments about the band's music and *New York Times* music critic Jon Pareles refers to Coldplay as "the most insufferable band of the decade." These views, however, are in the minority. In fact, according to Dave Tallis of the British Broadcasting Corporation, whose opinion may be more reflective of popular opinion, their third album is an undeniable masterpiece. He writes, "This album is superb. It'll silence their critics, amaze their fans and win them a whole new legion of admirers. It might even bring about world peace!"

_____ Not everyone adores them.

_____ Coldplay is "the most insufferable band of the decade."

_____ Their third album is an undeniable masterpiece.

_____ This album is superb.

◆ Reread paragraph 7 in the article. Write **one** statement from the paragraph that shows someone's opinion. Then write the clue words from the statement.

2. Opinion: _____

Clue words: _____

_____ Number of Correct Answers: Part B

C Using Words

◆ Complete each sentence with a word from the box. Write the missing word on the line.

effusive	**banter**	**accolades**
insufferable	**integrity**	

1. Her decision to tell the truth showed she had great

_____.

2. Sitting through the long, boring movie was _____.

3. The _____ between the two comedians continued throughout the show.

4. She told a personal story with _____ emotion.

5. The dance group received _____ for their skilled performance.

◆ Choose one word from the box. Write a new sentence using the word.

6. word: _____

_____

_____ Number of Correct Answers: Part C

D Writing About It

Write an Advertisement

◆ Write an advertisement for a Coldplay concert. Include information that will make readers want to attend the concert. Write **at least four** sentences. Use the checklist on page 103 to check your work.

See Coldplay Live in Concert!

_____

_____

_____

_____

_____

_____

Lesson 2 Add your correct answers from parts A, B, and C to get your total score. Then find the percentage for your total score on the chart below. Record your percentage on the graph on page 105.

_____ Total Score for Parts A, B, and C

_____ Percentage

Total Score	1	2	3	4	5	6	7	8	9	10	11	12	13
Percentage	8	15	23	31	38	46	54	62	69	77	85	92	100

Lisa Fernandez

Pushing the Limits

Birth Name Lisa Fernandez

Birth Date and Place February 22, 1971; Lakewood, California

Home Long Beach, California

Think About What You Know

Have you ever wanted to achieve a difficult goal? Did other people encourage you? Read the article to find out how softball pitcher Lisa Fernandez received both encouragement and criticism during her life.

Word Power

What do the words below tell you about the article?

tenacity a state of not giving up when trying to reach a goal or desired outcome

cajoling gently persuading someone with soothing talk and promises

compiling collecting or putting together

reconvened met or came together again

pivotal of central importance

Reading Skill

Drawing Conclusions Good readers **draw conclusions.** They combine information from several parts of the article with what they already know to find a bigger idea. As you read, look for details in the text that provide clues about the people and events in the article. Then, when you draw a conclusion, make sure it is supported by at least two clues in the text.

Example

There are two kinds of softball: slowpitch and fastpitch. In slowpitch softball, the pitcher always throws underhand, giving the ball a high arch. In fastpitch softball, there are many different types of pitches. The pitcher may throw a fastball, a curveball, a change-up, a drop ball, and many more.

What do you already know about talented athletes? One thing you might know is that *talented athletes usually look for sports that will challenge them.* So a conclusion that you might draw from this paragraph is that *skilled pitchers probably prefer fastpitch softball to slowpitch softball.* What are two clues from the paragraph that support this conclusion?

Lisa Fernandez

Pushing the Limits

Lisa Fernandez is frequently asked what advice she would give young athletes. "People in life are going to tell you what you can and can't do," she responds, "but really there's only one person who can limit you—and that's yourself. You have to learn how to keep going and create your own destiny."

2   Fernandez bases her advice on personal experience. When she pitched in her first softball game at age eight, it wasn't a pretty sight. "I hit 20 and walked about 20," she recalls, adding, "I think we lost 20 to 0." But as she points out, "In the next game, I made sure I only walked 18, and slowly but surely I developed into the pitcher I am now."

3   That kind of **tenacity** has helped make Fernandez into the greatest softball player in the world today. As a pitcher for the University of California, Los Angeles (UCLA), she broke seven school records, was a four-time All-American, and led the nation in both hitting and Earned Run Average (ERA). After college, she went on to be named the Amateur Softball Association's fast-pitch champion six times. She also won multiple gold medals in the Olympics, Pan-American Games, and International Softball Federation Championships.

4   Fernandez's athletic ability was evident at an early age, and she began playing softball when she was just four years old. She loved to practice in the California sun, but even bad weather didn't stop her: she simply moved indoors, using rolled-up socks as balls and **cajoling** her parents into throwing them to her.

5   Fernandez was lucky to have the support of her parents, both of whom were knowledgeable about softball and pleased by their daughter's interest in the game. Fernandez's father, Tony, had played semi-professional baseball in Cuba before coming to the United States. "When I was growing up," Lisa says, "it wasn't really the most

acceptable thing to have a Hispanic daughter playing athletics and I can't say enough about my dad and his support of me. He never said, 'You shouldn't do that, that's not ladylike.'"

6   Fernandez also credits her mother, Emilia, who had played softball in her native Puerto Rico and was happy to help Lisa develop her pitching skills by serving as catcher during informal practice sessions in the family's backyard. Initially Emilia used a regular fielding glove, but as Lisa's pitches got stronger and faster, she switched to a catcher's glove, eventually adding a face mask, chest pad, and shin guards. By the time Lisa was 11, Emilia no longer dared catch for her. Lisa's pitches were simply too hot to handle. Soon her parents had to hire a private pitching instructor.

7   Although Fernandez showed tremendous promise, some people scoffed at the idea of her pursuing softball in a serious way. One coach told her that she ran "like a turkey" and another said she would never be a successful softball pitcher because she didn't have "the right body type." Fernandez didn't believe any of that. By the age of 12, she began to believe that her future *did* lie with softball. This thought came to her while she sat in her living room watching UCLA play Nebraska in the first nationally televised Women's College World Series. It was, she says, "the first time I said, 'Softball can take me somewhere.'"

8   As a teenager, Fernandez established herself as the star pitcher for Lakewood's St. Joseph High School, **compiling** a record of 80 victories, including 69 no-hitters, 39 shutouts, and 12 perfect games.

Skill Break

Drawing Conclusions

Look at paragraph 7 on this page. The paragraph describes some of Fernandez's early experiences as a softball player. One **conclusion** the reader might draw from the paragraph is that *the coaches judged Fernandez's potential skills based on the way she looked.*

Can you find **two clues** in the text that support this conclusion?

How does **what you already know** support this conclusion?

Perhaps her most memorable high school game came freshman year, when St. Joseph faced Gahr High School. Fernandez came onto the field throwing fire; the opposing pitcher, a girl named DeDe Weiman, did the same. For 21 scoreless innings these two pitchers battled it out, until the sun had set and it was too dark to see the ball. Officials suspended the game until the next day, when the two teams **reconvened** to finish up. Finally, after eight more scoreless innings, Fernandez scored a run for her team, securing a 1-0 win. It had been a fierce struggle and emotions ran high. The St. Joseph players were ecstatic; the Gahr girls were in tears.

9   While Fernandez was thrilled to have won, she demonstrated classic sportsmanship by taking the time to show her respect for the opposing pitcher. DeDe Weiman recalls, "Lisa came and hugged me, and said, 'There's no winner or loser here.'"

10   Fernandez gave more dazzling performances and accumulated more incredible statistics in college and later as a member of various amateur teams. Then in 1996 a new opportunity arose. Softball was added to the Olympic Games and Fernandez became a **pivotal** player on the U.S. team. During the 1996 Games, she posted 31 strikeouts over 21 innings and was acknowledged for protecting her team's lead in the gold-medal game against Canada.

11   Four years later, Fernandez was back at the Olympics. This time the U.S. team got off to a rocky start, losing three games in the preliminary round before settling in to win the next five in a row. In the semifinal game, Fernandez pitched the full seven innings to defeat Australia, 1-0. Less than 24 hours later, she was on the mound again,

Fun Facts

▶ Fernandez enjoys playing golf.
▶ When she was at UCLA she played both softball and basketball.

▶ She can pitch a softball as fast as 69 miles per hour. The world record is 71 miles per hour.

Lisa Fernandez winds up for a pitch during the championship series of the 2004 Olympic Games.

this time facing Japan in the finals. With so little rest for her arm, Fernandez knew it would be a struggle. But Coach Ralph Raymond had no doubts about using her two days in a row. In fact he said he'd use her *three* days in a row if necessary, declaring, "That's the kind of talent she has." Raymond's faith in Fernandez proved justified: despite her fatigue, she pitched the complete game for a 2-1 victory and a second gold medal.

12   In 2004 Fernandez entered her third consecutive Olympic competition. This time the United States blew away the opposition in stunning fashion, winning nine games by a combined score of 51 to 1. Australia managed to score one run in the championship game, but lost anyway, 5-1. Once again Fernandez pitched the final two games, leading the U.S. women to a third consecutive Olympic championship.

13   Afterwards the 33-year-old Fernandez left open the possibility of a fourth or even fifth Olympic appearance. "Thus far I've had no injuries, no problems," she says. "If I can feel this way in 2008, maybe even 2012 won't be out of the question." No doubt remembering the advice she dispenses to young athletes, she adds, "I'm never going to put a limit on myself."

A Understanding What You Read

◆ **Fill in the circle next to the correct answer.**

1. In her most memorable high school game, Fernandez

○ A. faced opposing pitcher DeDe Weiman.

○ B. did not have enough time to rest her arm.

○ C. followed the advice of her pitching coach.

2. Which of the following statements is an opinion rather than a fact?

○ A. She was named fast-pitch champion.

○ B. The family hired a pitching instructor.

○ C. There's no winner or loser here.

3. Fernandez's first chance to go to the Olympics came in 1996 because

○ A. the Canadians asked her to pitch on their team.

○ B. she didn't graduate from high school until 1996.

○ C. softball wasn't an Olympic sport before 1996.

4. How is Lisa Fernandez an example of an experienced athlete?

○ A. She has no plans to retire from softball.

○ B. She has been to the Olympics three times.

○ C. Her parents are both strong athletes.

5. Which sentence **best** states the lesson about life that this article teaches?

○ A. Winning requires patience and sacrifice.

○ B. Don't put unnecessary limits on yourself.

○ C. Listen carefully to what people tell you.

_____ Number of Correct Answers: Part A

B Drawing Conclusions

◆ Read the paragraph below. Fill in the circle next to the conclusion that is **best** supported by the clues in the paragraph.

1.

Four years later, Fernandez was back at the Olympics. This time the U.S. team got off to a rocky start, losing three games in the preliminary round before settling in to win the next five in a row. In the semifinal game, Fernandez pitched the full seven innings to defeat Australia, 1-0. Less than 24 hours later, she was on the mound again, this time facing Japan in the finals. With so little rest for her arm, Fernandez knew it would be a struggle. But Coach Ralph Raymond had no doubts about using her two days in a row. In fact he said he'd use her *three* days in a row if necessary, declaring, "That's the kind of talent she has." Raymond's faith in Fernandez proved justified: despite her fatigue, she pitched the complete game for a 2-1 victory and a second gold medal.

○ A. Fernandez didn't want to overwork her arm.
○ B. Fernandez can play well even when she is tired.
○ C. Fernandez pitches her best at the end of a game.

◆ What clues from the paragraph support this conclusion? Write **two** clues from the paragraph. Then explain how what you already know helped you draw this conclusion.

2. Clue: _____

Clue: _____

What I Know: _____

_____

_____ Number of Correct Answers: Part B

C Using Words

◆ Complete the analogies below by writing a word from the box on each line. Remember that in an analogy, the last two words or phrases must be related in the same way that the first two are related.

tenacity	compiling	pivotal
cajoling	reconvened	

1. drawing : doodling :: asking : _____

2. stiff : flexible :: weakness : _____

3. firewood : gathering :: information : _____

4. funny : comical :: essential : _____

5. remove : replace :: scattered : _____

◆ Choose one word from the box. Write a sentence using the word.

6. word: _____

_____

_____

_____ Number of Correct Answers: Part C

D Writing About It

Write Interview Questions

◆ Suppose you have a chance to interview Lisa Fernandez. Write **four** questions you would like to ask. Use the checklist on page 103 to check your work.

1. _____

   _____

2. _____

   _____

3. _____

   _____

4. _____

   _____

Lesson 3 Add your correct answers from parts A, B, and C to get your total score. Then find the percentage for your total score on the chart below. Record your percentage on the graph on page 105.

_____ Total Score for Parts A, B, and C

_____ Percentage

Total Score	1	2	3	4	5	6	7	8	9	10	11	12	13
Percentage	8	15	23	31	38	46	54	62	69	77	85	92	100

Compare and Contrast

◆ Think about the celebrities in Unit One. Pick two articles that tell about celebrities who set very high standards for themselves. Use information from the articles to fill in this chart.

Celebrity's or Group's Name		
What are the celebrity's or group's high standards?		
What does the celebrity or group do to show or maintain those high standards?		
What is the result?		

Unit 2

Manu Ginobili

Oprah Winfrey

Rulon Gardner

Manu Ginobili

Basketball Wizard

Birth Name Emanuel David Ginobili

Birth Date and Place July 28, 1977; Bahia Blanca, Argentina

Homes San Antonio, Texas, and Bahia Blanca, Argentina

Think About What You Know

Have you ever chosen to do something that was unpopular with the majority of the people in your town—or even your country? Read the article to find out how Manu Ginobili became a basketball star in a country of soccer players.

Word Power

What do the words below tell you about the article?

integral necessary to the completeness of the whole

memorabilia objects valued for their connection with a particular person, event, or interest

adulation exaggerated praise or flattery

maraca a rattle-like musical instrument made from a hollow gourd containing seeds or pebbles

echelon a particular level of authority or responsibility

Reading Skill

Asking Questions to Get Information Good readers **ask questions.** Asking and answering questions as you read can help you find the most important ideas in the text. Make sure to ask questions about the big ideas. Asking questions that start with *what, where, when, how,* and *why* can help you find the big ideas.

Example

While there are many popular sports in Argentina, such as polo, skiing, and tennis, Argentina's national sport is soccer. Soccer has been played in Argentina since the British first introduced the game there in the 1800s. The Argentina national team has won the World Cup of soccer a number of times, most recently in 1986.

"*Why* is soccer so popular in Argentina?" is one question you might ask yourself to help you find important information in this paragraph. Why do you think this is such a good question to ask about this paragraph?

Manu Ginobili

Basketball Wizard

When the words "Argentina" and "athlete" appear together in the same sentence, the subject under discussion is usually a soccer player. But there is one notable exception to this rule: Emanuel "Manu" Ginobili, one of the most dynamic players in today's National Basketball Association (NBA). With his flashy, whirling, explosive style of play, Ginobili has helped lead the San Antonio Spurs to NBA championships in 2003 and 2005 and has captured the imagination of sports fans all over the world.

2   Ginobili was born and raised in Bahia Blanca, an Argentinean city of 290,000 people located about 350 miles southwest of Buenos Aires. It is the only basketball stronghold in Argentina, boasting more than 20 organized basketball clubs and 150 different teams.

3   Like his two older brothers, Ginobili embraced this local pastime, learning the proper way to dribble (eyes up with your free hand out to the side to prevent steals) when he was just three years old. Even though he practiced his ball-handling skills for hours each day and had boundless enthusiasm for the game, Ginobili did not appear to be a particularly gifted player. When he was 15 years old, he still wasn't good enough to earn a spot on the city's All-Star team, although he had friends his age who were.

4   The problem was mostly his size. Ginobili was a skinny kid with underdeveloped muscles and no great height advantage. Luckily, however, he was also a kid who wasn't easily discouraged, so he stayed with basketball even when it didn't look like he had much of a future in big-league play. Because he was too small to play under the basket where the big players congregated, he developed an excellent outside shot, focusing especially on three-pointers.

5   Then to his delight, Ginobili hit a growth spurt, sprouting to six feet, six inches and adding some bulk to his frame. He became stronger, and suddenly he didn't have to settle for outside shots anymore. All that dribbling practice over the years paid off as Ginobili raced down the court with ease, using his increased size and strength to drive to the basket against even the toughest opponents. As his offensive game blossomed, so did his defensive skills. He became a master at stealing the ball and fought doggedly for every ball that got loose.

6   Ginobili improved so much that in 1995 he joined a professional league in Argentina and three years later moved to a more competitive league in Italy. There he caught the attention of the San Antonio Spurs, who selected him as their second-round pick in the 1999 NBA draft. Ginobili didn't join the Spurs right away, however; he stayed in Italy for three more years to gain additional experience.

7   This proved to be an excellent strategy as he was named the Italian League's Most Valuable Player (MVP) in both 2001 and 2002. In addition, in the summer of 2002, Ginobili played on Argentina's national team at the World Basketball Championship. The Argentines didn't win the championship but they did finish second, scoring an upset victory over the United States along the way. That was enough to earn Ginobili star status back in Bahia Blanca, and he was treated like a regional hero when he returned there to visit his family.

8   By the 2002–2003 season, the Spurs felt confident that Ginobili was ready for the NBA so they brought him to San Antonio, where he quickly established himself as an **integral** member of the team.

Skill Break

Asking Questions to Get Information

Look at paragraph 6 on this page. The paragraph describes what happened when Ginobili began to play basketball professionally.

What would be a good **question** to ask to find the **important information** in this paragraph?

What is the **answer** to your question?

That season Ginobili helped the Spurs win the NBA championship. In the 2003–2004 season he played even better, with an improved scoring average and more steals than anyone on the team. As a reward, the San Antonio Spurs signed him to a new six-year, $52 million contract.

9   Ginobili enjoyed his success in the NBA, but the ultimate thrill came in the 2004 off-season, when he donned a jersey for Argentina's Olympic basketball team. The rest of the team was comprised of relative unknowns, with names that most U.S. basketball fans didn't recognize. Even in Argentina, few people thought this team had much of a chance to win the gold medal. After all, the country hadn't won a gold medal in any Summer Olympic sport in over 50 years, and there was little reason to believe this year would be different. Fans soon found out, however, that they had been underestimating this group of players, failing to anticipate how seamlessly they would work together and how much energy Manu Ginobili would bring to the team.

10   Throughout the series Ginobili was a whirlwind on the court, passing, rebounding, stealing the ball—and averaging almost 20 points a game. Under his leadership, the Argentines won game after game. They even defeated the U.S. team, which was filled with big-name NBA players, and then the Argentines went right on to beat Italy, securing the gold medal. It was no surprise when Ginobili was named the MVP after the championship game.

11   Having ended Argentina's long gold-medal drought, Ginobili became a bigger hero in his homeland than ever before. The entire country became swept up in "Manu Mania," with thousands of fans waiting in lines to request his autograph and countless more buying jerseys, posters, and other **memorabilia** bearing his name.

Fun Facts

▶ Ginobili likes to surf the Internet.

▶ When he met his idol, Michael Jordan, Ginobili admits he "shivered a little bit."

▶ Besides Manu, his other nicknames include Gino and Narigón, which means "big nose" in Spanish.

Manu Ginobili goes up for the shot during a game against the Denver Nuggets.

Thanks to Ginobili, basketball was suddenly viewed as a big-time sport in Argentina. "Because of Manu, it is an explosion and a magic all over the country," declared Juan Carlos Meschini, a television sports commentator. "Many people who saw basketball as something distant, different from soccer, are coming around to the sport."

12   Ginobili might have let all this **adulation** go to his head, but instead he remains the same modest, humble person he has always been. At least, that's his personality *off* the court. When he's in a basketball game, Ginobili is a different creature altogether.

13   "The one thing you notice, right off the bat," says teammate Brent Barry, "is the energy Manu plays with."

14   Teammate Robert Horry adds that Ginobili is "always going hard, always diving, jumping, doing whatever he has to do."

15   Perhaps that's why Ginobili has been called everything from a circus entertainer to a "human **maraca.**" With his wild, sprawling dives for the ball and behind-the-back dribbles, he excites the crowd and disarms his opponents. "He belongs in the top **echelon** of players on this planet," says Spurs coach Gregg Popovich. And basketball fans around the globe look forward to Manu Ginobili continuing to make his moves for years to come.

A Understanding What You Read

◆ Fill in the circle next to the correct answer.

1. Why did Ginobili need to become very good at making outside shots?

- ○ A. He needed to adjust for his weak defensive skills.
- ○ B. He was too small to play under the basket.
- ○ C. His dribbling technique was not strong enough.

2. From what you read in the article, which of these is probably true?

- ○ A. A number of NBA players used to play on European teams.
- ○ B. Basketball will soon become Argentina's national sport.
- ○ C. South America doesn't have professional basketball teams.

3. In 2004 no one expected Argentina to win an Olympic gold medal because

- ○ A. U.S. basketball fans didn't know any Argentine players.
- ○ B. Ginobili hadn't done very well with the San Antonio Spurs.
- ○ C. Argentina hadn't won an Olympic gold medal in a long time.

4. If you were a travel agent in Argentina, how could you use the information in the article to attract tourists?

- ○ A. I would lead a tour of Bahia Blanca, Ginobili's hometown.
- ○ B. I would offer free NBA tickets with every travel package.
- ○ C. I would create trips to see sporting events in Argentina.

5. Which sentence **best** states the main idea of the article?

- ○ A. Ginobili helped Argentina win an Olympic championship.
- ○ B. Ginobili's hometown has many enthusiastic basketball fans.
- ○ C. Ginobili is a unique and extraordinary basketball talent.

_____ Number of Correct Answers: Part A

B Asking Questions to Get Information

◆ Read the paragraph below. Fill in the circle next to the **best** question to ask to find important information in the paragraph.

1.

Having ended Argentina's long gold-medal drought, Ginobili became a bigger hero in his homeland than ever before. The entire country became swept up in "Manu Mania," with thousands of fans waiting in lines to request his autograph and countless more buying jerseys, posters, and other memorabilia bearing his name. Thanks to Ginobili, basketball was suddenly viewed as a big-time sport in Argentina. "Because of Manu, it is an explosion and a magic all over the country," declared Juan Carlos Meschini, a television sports commentator. "Many people who saw basketball as something distant, different from soccer, are coming around to the sport."

○ A. When did fans in Argentina want to buy memorabilia with Ginobili's name on it?

○ B. What did a television sports commentator say to Ginobili after the Olympics?

○ C. Why did winning a gold medal change many Argentines' minds about basketball?

◆ Reread paragraphs 13 to 15 in the article. Write **one** question that would help you find the most important information in the paragraphs. Then write the answer to your question.

2. Question: _____

_____

Answer: _____

_____ Number of Correct Answers: Part B

41

C Using Words

◆ The words in the list below relate to the words in the box. Some words in the list have the same meaning or a similar meaning as a word in the box. Some have the opposite meaning. Write the related word from the box on each line. Use each word from the box twice.

integral	adulation	echelon
memorabilia	maraca	

Same or similar meaning

1. compliments _____

2. instrument _____

3. ranking _____

4. essential _____

5. level _____

6. souvenirs _____

7. rattle _____

8. reminders _____

Opposite meaning

9. ridicule _____

10. unimportant _____

_____ Number of Correct Answers: Part C

D Writing About It

Write a News Article

◆ Suppose you were a reporter covering basketball at the 2004 Olympics. Write an article about Argentina winning the gold medal. Be sure to include information about Ginobili's role in Argentina's victory. Write **at least four** sentences. Use the checklist on page 103 to check your work.

_____

_____

_____

_____

_____

_____

_____

Lesson 4 Add your correct answers from parts A, B, and C to get your total score. Then find the percentage for your total score on the chart below. Record your percentage on the graph on page 105.

_____ Total Score for Parts A, B, and C

_____ Percentage

Total Score	1	2	3	4	5	6	7	8	9	10	11	12	13	14	15	16	17
Percentage	6	12	18	24	29	35	41	47	53	59	65	70	76	82	88	94	100

Oprah Winfrey

Rising Above, Reaching Out

Birth Name Orpah Gail Winfrey

Birth Date and Place January 29, 1954; Kosciusko, Mississippi

Homes Chicago, Illinois, and several other cities

Think About What You Know

If you became one of the wealthiest people in the world, how would you use your money? Read the article and find out how Oprah Winfrey uses her wealth and influence.

Word Power

What do the words below tell you about the article?

impoverished very poor

instilled introduced or taught something over a period of time

demoted reduced to a lower rank

syndication a system of selling a television show to many different stations

accessibility openness or approachability

Reading Skill

Fact and Opinion A **fact** is a statement that can be proved by checking a research source. An **opinion** is someone's own idea or belief about something. When a statement includes words that show judgment, such as *best, should, excellent,* or *amazing,* that statement usually contains someone's opinion. When authors state an opinion in their writing, they usually support the opinion with facts.

Example

Opinion The Oprah Winfrey Foundation is a very good charity organization. The foundation tries to address areas of great

Fact need around the world. For example, the foundation donated 10 million dollars to create a leadership academy for girls in South Africa.

In this paragraph, the author's opinion is that "The Oprah Winfrey Foundation is a very good charity organization." The author supports this opinion by stating a fact about the girls' leadership academy in South Africa. How does this fact support the author's opinion?

Oprah Winfrey

Rising Above, Reaching Out

She doesn't have a business degree, she has never taken an acting class, and she suffered through an **impoverished,** unstable childhood that included an abusive home life. Nonetheless, Oprah Winfrey's talents have propelled her toward resounding success and allowed her to establish a solid place for herself at the very top of the business and entertainment worlds. Not only does she have the most popular talk show in the history of television, but she also owns her own production company, has founded her own magazine, and has been nominated for an Academy Award. And along the way, she has become one of the wealthiest people on the planet.

2   Winfrey was born in 1954 in Kosciusko, Mississippi, to 18-year-old Vernita Lee. Winfrey's parents were never married, and they split up when she was a baby. As a small child Winfrey lived with her grandmother, who **instilled** in her a love of books and a sense that she was special, but at age six she was sent to Milwaukee, Wisconsin, to live with her mother. Winfrey has talked candidly about how difficult life was for her in her mother's home, where she was sexually abused by relatives and by her mother's male friends. She became confused and rebellious, frequently getting into trouble for telling lies, stealing from her mother's purse, breaking curfew, and running away.

3   At age 14, after her mother tried unsuccessfully to place her in a detention home, Oprah was sent to Nashville, Tennessee, to live with her father, Vernon Winfrey, who provided a very different environment. Her father insisted that she respect his values, follow his strict rules, and read at least one book a week. Oprah eventually responded to her father's approach, and by the time she was 19 she had salvaged her self-esteem and her future. She gained admission to Tennessee State University and secured a job as a reporter for

a local radio station, eventually working her way up to become anchorwoman of a television news show in Baltimore, Maryland.

4   Winfrey was a fine anchorwoman and her ratings were good, but she received hate mail from racist viewers who didn't like the idea of an African American woman delivering the news. Even her bosses felt that she looked a little too "ethnic," telling her that her hair was too thick, her nose was too wide, and her chin was too big. They also thought she was too emotional. On top of that, they didn't think she was thin enough. Soon she was **demoted** from anchorwoman and given a job as the host of a morning talk show called *People Are Talking*.

5   This "demotion" turned out to be the best thing that could have happened to Winfrey. Being an anchorwoman hadn't allowed all of her warmth and intelligence to show through, but in a talk show setting she was free to be natural and relaxed. In this new role her wit and compassion became valuable assets, and she used them to connect with viewers on a deeper, more personal level.

6   In 1984, finally realizing how talented Winfrey was, network executives transferred her from Baltimore to a much bigger station in Chicago, where she took over a little-known morning talk show called A.M. *Chicago*. Within one month she had transformed it into a hit show. Soon, the program was renamed *The Oprah Winfrey Show* and was put into **syndication,** quickly expanding to more than 120 cities across the United States. By the next year, Winfrey's show was the top talk show in the country, watched by 10 million people daily.

Skill Break

Fact and Opinion

Look at paragraphs 5 and 6 on this page. In the first sentence of paragraph 5, the author writes that Winfrey's demotion was the best thing that could have happened to her. Although most people might agree with this statement, it is an **opinion** because *it shows a judgment*. It is not a fact because *it cannot be proved*.

What information does the author provide in paragraphs 5 and 6 to **support** this opinion about Winfrey's demotion?

7   More than 20 years later, Winfrey is still the reigning queen of daytime talk shows, discussing everything from gun control to AIDS to her own efforts at weight loss. No matter what the topic, Winfrey has proven herself to be insightful and understanding, with an appealing mix of toughness, humor, and sensitivity. One viewer explained Winfrey's popularity this way: "People are in awe of Oprah, but at the same time we feel like she could be our best friend." It's that blend of talent and **accessibility** that has helped Oprah become a household name.

8   Once she reached the top of her profession, Winfrey found herself in a position of tremendous financial power and networking resources; she has used her wealth and resources to give financial support to hundreds of worthy causes. In 1997 she started Oprah's Angel Network, which has donated millions of dollars to schools, hospitals, and community projects from China to Africa to the United States. Beyond that, the Network gives out "Use Your Life" awards of $10,000 to people who are devoting their lives to helping others.

9   Some of Winfrey's actions are astonishing in their size and range. In December of 2002, she made an incredible donation to the people of South Africa, giving millions of dollars to help fund clinics, schools, and orphanages there. She also spent three weeks in South Africa handing out presents to 50,000 needy children. On the opening show of her 2004 season, Winfrey once again gave out gifts, this time to members of her studio audience. During the show, Winfrey brought 11 people onto the stage and gave them each a brand new car. She then distributed boxes to the other 265 members of the audience, announcing that one of the boxes contained a key for a 12th car.

Fun Facts

▶ Winfrey's mother named her "Orpah," which was repeatedly misspelled and became "Oprah."

▶ She learned to read when she was two-and-a-half years old.

▶ At the beginning of kindergarten she wrote a note to her teacher explaining why she should be in first grade. After reading the note, her teacher agreed.

Oprah Winfrey poses with Nelson Mandela at the ground-breaking ceremony for the Oprah Winfrey Leadership Academy for Girls—South Africa.

In reality, all the boxes contained a key and moments later Winfrey proclaimed, "Everybody gets a car!" For Winfrey this wasn't just a publicity stunt; she made sure that each person invited into the studio that day was truly in need of a new vehicle.

10   Winfrey has made other contributions that have been equally impressive. She has become a champion of literacy, and by selecting a book each month to discuss for Oprah's Book Club, she has helped propel dozens of books to the bestseller list. Winfrey has also created a magazine called *O, The Oprah Magazine,* which features articles aimed at helping women improve their self-esteem and lead healthier lives. In addition, the acting roles she has accepted over the years have showcased strong characters coping with difficult situations.

11   Oprah Winfrey has become the very definition of success, so it's little wonder that in 2005, *Forbes* magazine named her the most powerful celebrity on Earth and placed her 507th among the World's Richest Business Leaders. Still, Winfrey hasn't let success destroy her humility. "Believe me," she told one reporter, "my feet are still on the ground." Then she paused and added, "I'm just wearing better shoes."

A Understanding What You Read

◆ Fill in the circle next to the correct answer or write the answer.

1. The most difficult time in Winfrey's childhood was when she lived in

   ○ A. Kosciusko, Mississippi.
   ○ B. Milwaukee, Wisconsin.
   ○ C. Nashville, Tennessee.

2. Choose from the letters below to correctly complete the following statement. Write the letters on the lines.

   On the negative side, _____, but on the positive side, _____.

   A. Oprah did very well as a talk show host
   B. Oprah was demoted from anchorwoman
   C. Oprah went to college and graduated

3. Oprah's Angel Network contributes money for

   ○ A. gifts to her studio audience.
   ○ B. community projects around the world.
   ○ C. student scholarships in journalism.

4. In which paragraph did you find the information to answer question 3?

   _____

5. From the information in the article, you can predict that Winfrey will

   ○ A. donate more money to South Africa.
   ○ B. be demoted from talk show host.
   ○ C. refuse to read *Forbes* magazine.

_____ Number of Correct Answers: Part A

B Understanding Fact and Opinion

◆ Reread paragraph 9 in the article. Write the letter *O* on the lines
next to the statements that show someone's opinion. Write the
letter *F* on the lines next to the statements that are facts.

1.

_____ Some of Winfrey's actions are astonishing in their size and range.

_____ She made an incredible donation to the people of South Africa.

_____ She gave millions of dollars to help fund clinics, schools, and
orphanages.

_____ In 2004 Winfrey gave new cars to all 276 people in her studio audience.

◆ Reread paragraph 10 in the article. Write the author's opinion.
Then write **one** piece of information that supports this opinion.
Explain whether the supporting information is a fact or an opinion.

2. Author's Opinion: _____

_____

Supporting Information: _____

_____

Fact or Opinion? _____

_____

_____ Number of Correct Answers: Part B

Using Words

◆ Complete each sentence with a word from the box. Write the
missing word on the line.

impoverished	demoted	accessibility
instilled	syndication	

1. She was _____ for poor job performance.

2. His music teacher _____ in him a love of Mozart.

3. The _____ immigrants did not have enough to eat.

4. Because of its _____, the TV show could be viewed in
every major city in the Midwest.

5. The teacher's friendliness and _____ made him a
favorite with students.

◆ Choose one of the words from the box. Write a new sentence
using the word.

6. word: _____

_____

_____

_____ Number of Correct Answers: Part C

 **Writing About It**

Write a Postcard

◆ Suppose you were in the studio when Oprah gave away cars to everyone in the audience. Write a postcard to a friend describing what happened. Write **at least four** sentences. Use the checklist on page 103 to check your work.

Dear _____,

_____

_____

_____

_____

_____

_____

Your friend,

_____

789 Pal Rd.
Hometown, USA

Lesson 5 Add your correct answers from parts A, B, and C to get your total score. Then find the percentage for your total score on the chart below. Record your percentage on the graph on page 105.

_____ Total Score for Parts A, B, and C

_____ Percentage

Total Score	1	2	3	4	5	6	7	8	9	10	11	12	13
Percentage	8	15	23	31	38	46	54	62	69	77	85	92	100

Rulon Gardner

A Long, Hard Journey

Birth Name Rulon Ellis Gardner

Birth Date and Place August 16, 1971; Afton, Wyoming

Home Wellsville, Utah

Think About What You Know

Have you ever seen a high school or college wrestling match? What did you notice about how wrestlers use their bodies? Read the article and find out about Rulon Gardner's career as an Olympic wrestler.

Word Power

What do the words below tell you about the article?

precludes prevents someone from doing something

hypothermia a condition of dangerously low body temperature caused by being in the cold too long

oblivion a state of unconsciousness

minute very small

acquitting behaving in a certain way

Reading Skill

Drawing Conclusions Good readers **draw conclusions.** They combine information from several parts of an article with what they already know to find a bigger idea. As you read, look for details in the text that provide clues about the people and events in the article. Evaluate the clues carefully. Your conclusions should be supported by at least two clues in the text.

Example

Wrestling became part of the ancient Olympics starting in 706 B.C. But wrestling was practiced as a sport long before the ancient Olympics began. Wrestlers are shown in ancient Egyptian wall paintings that date to around 2400 B.C. Cave drawings that show people wrestling date back as far as 3000 B.C.

What do you already know about sports and history? One thing you might know is that *the sports played at the ancient Olympics are some of the oldest sports in the world.* So a conclusion that you might draw from this paragraph is that *wrestling is one of the oldest sports in the world.* What are two clues from the paragraph that support this conclusion?

Rulon Gardner

A Long, Hard Journey

Heading into the 2000 Olympics, Rulon Gardner was, in his own words, a "no one from Wyoming." The youngest of nine children, he had been raised on a dairy farm, where he spent much of his time lifting bales of hay and wrestling his brothers to see who would have to do the least desirable chores. Although Gardner was the best Greco-Roman wrestler in the United States, no one really thought he stood a chance against the great Alexander Karelin, a legendary Russian who was said to train by hauling logs through the Siberian winter and who had not been defeated in 13 years. So when Gardner beat Karelin to win the Olympic gold medal, the wrestling world exploded with shock and excitement. The experts agreed that Gardner had reached the height of his career. What they didn't know—what no one knew—was that Gardner's most difficult and inspiring journey was still ahead of him.

2   After winning the gold medal, Gardner returned to his hometown of Afton, Wyoming, to train for more international competitions. Like all Greco-Roman wrestlers, he needed tremendous strength, endurance, and balance to perform well. Greco-Roman wrestlers adhere to a version of the sport developed in ancient Greece, which forbids participants from using their legs to topple an opponent and **precludes** them from using any holds below the waist. At 286 pounds, Gardner competed in the super heavyweight division; he hoped he'd still be there when the 2004 Olympics rolled around. His career seemed right on track when, in 2001, he won the World Championship and was awarded the James E. Sullivan Award for athletic excellence, leadership, sportsmanship, and character. But on February 14, 2002, his future took an unexpected detour.

3   The day started out pleasantly enough, with Gardner and two friends hopping on snowmobiles to explore Cottonwood Canyon, a

starkly beautiful section of Wyoming's Bridger-Teton National Forest. By 4:00 P.M. the other two men had turned back, but Gardner forged ahead, hoping to make it to the top of Wagner Mountain before heading home. About half an hour later he entered a gully so steep and narrow that he couldn't have turned around even if he'd tried. He wasn't particularly concerned, though. He figured that if he kept going he'd end up at Salt River and could then follow the riverbed back to familiar territory. Unfortunately, as he tried to navigate the gully, his snowmobile crashed through a weak spot in the snow and dropped seven feet into a shallow stream below.

4   It took all of Gardner's substantial strength to extract the 650-pound vehicle from the stream, and by the time he'd done that he was wet up to his thighs and perspiring heavily. With night falling and the temperature dropping rapidly, the conditions were perfect for the onset of **hypothermia.**

5   Stubbornly and with perhaps a hint of panic, Gardner climbed back on the snowmobile and continued driving. The next gully surprised him, and this time the drop was much larger. Unable to see clearly in the gathering darkness, he drove his snowmobile right off a 50-foot cliff. Gardner remarkably survived the fall, but his snowmobile was ruined. He had to continue on foot, plowing his way through waist-high snow until finally he sank down, exhausted, amidst a small stand of trees.

6   For the next ten hours, Gardner struggled to stay awake as heat seeped out of his body and he got closer to **oblivion.** Much of what kept him going through that long night of subzero temperatures were thoughts of the things he loved: his family, his girlfriend, and wrestling.

Skill Break
Drawing Conclusions

Look at paragraph 4 on this page. One conclusion the reader might draw from this paragraph is that *being wet increases the risk of hypothermia.*

Can you find at least **two clues** in the paragraph to support this conclusion?

How does **what you already know** support this conclusion?

7   About 10:00 A.M. the next morning, a rescue helicopter plucked Gardner out of the snow and rushed him to a hospital. By then his body temperature was so low that he hovered near death, but Gardner had luck on his side and somehow he survived. Still, the miscalculation he'd made on that frigid winter night cost him dearly. After battling for six weeks to save his frostbitten toes, doctors finally amputated Gardner's middle right toe and the tips of both big toes.

8   Most people would have counted their blessings that they hadn't lost anything more essential than toes, but to Gardner—to *any* Greco-Roman wrestler—toes are of critical importance. Toes help wrestlers maintain balance. They add stability to precarious stances and help wrestlers shift weight quickly. When Gardner learned he was losing a toe, he fell into despair. But because he was not ready to give up the sport he loved, he slowly and painfully began to stage a comeback.

9   Three months after the amputation Gardner could walk again, but he had to wear special open-toed shoes to accommodate the steel pins that kept his big toes from curling. Four months after that, the pins were removed and Gardner returned to the gym, spending two hours every day getting his strength back, regaining his balance, and learning to compensate for his stiff feet and missing toe. Amazingly, by 2003 he had returned to international competition. Gardner's return to the Olympics was far from certain, however, especially after he finished a disappointing 10th at the 2003 World Championship.

10   In the months just before the Olympic trials, Gardner was involved in a motorcycle crash, and narrowly escaped serious injury. Then he dislocated his wrist during a game of pick-up basketball, an injury

Fun Facts

- Gardner wears size 13 shoes.
- He still loves snowmobiling, and says, "I'd snowmobile every day if I could."
- He once won a bet with his coach by carrying a 215-pound teammate over his shoulder for more than a mile.

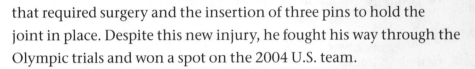

An emotional Rulon Gardner removes his wrestling shoes for the last time after his bronze-winning performance at the 2004 Olympics.

that required surgery and the insertion of three pins to hold the joint in place. Despite this new injury, he fought his way through the Olympic trials and won a spot on the 2004 U.S. team.

11   For Gardner, making the team was the realization of a dream that had seen him through his darkest hours. He knew he was heading into the competition with handicaps. "I can't sense every **minute** detail of what my toes are telling me," he said, also admitting that "there are some lingering effects of the dislocated wrist." But for Gardner, merely getting to the Olympics once again was a monumental victory. Beyond that, all he cared about was **acquitting** himself well during the competition. "I came here for personal satisfaction," he said. "I want to walk off the mat and know I've done my best."

12   That's just what he did. On August 25, 2004, Gardner won an Olympic bronze medal. Not only had he come back from a near-death accident, amputation, and other serious injuries, he had reclaimed his place as one of the top three wrestlers in the world.

13   When the match was over, he acted out the traditional farewell gesture of wrestlers everywhere. He unlaced his shoes and set them on the mat. Then with tears streaming down his face, Rulon Gardner walked off the mat and into retirement.

Understanding What You Read

◆ **Fill in the circle next to the correct answer.**

1. Why didn't Gardner turn around after he entered the gully in Cottonwood Canyon?

   ○ A. He was going too fast to turn around.
   ○ B. His snowmobile was stuck in the snow.
   ○ C. He didn't have enough room to turn around.

2. What was the effect of Gardner's losing a toe to frostbite?

   ○ A. He had to work harder to balance and shift his weight.
   ○ B. He had to be in the hospital for over six weeks.
   ○ C. He could no longer do Greco-Roman wrestling.

3. Why did Gardner remove his shoes at the 2004 Olympics?

   ○ A. to make a traditional farewell gesture
   ○ B. to soothe his sore feet after the match
   ○ C. to get ready to wrestle his next opponent

4. The author probably wrote this article in order to

   ○ A. teach the reader about different types of wrestling.
   ○ B. inform the reader about a remarkable athlete.
   ○ C. warn the reader about the dangers of snowmobiles.

5. Which of the following categories would this article **best** fit into?

   ○ A. Ways to Increase Your Strength
   ○ B. Things You Have to See to Believe
   ○ C. Stories of Survival and Recovery

_____ Number of Correct Answers: Part A

B Drawing Conclusions

◆ Read the conclusion below. Write the letter C on the line next to each clue that supports this conclusion.

1. **Conclusion:** Rulon Gardner is not a particularly cautious person.

_____ He wasn't very concerned about snowmobiling in a steep, narrow gully.

_____ He spent two hours at the gym every day getting his strength back.

_____ He narrowly escaped serious injury in a motorcycle crash just months before the Olympic trials.

_____ He dislocated his wrist playing basketball and had to have surgery.

_____ He took off his shoes and left them on the mat during the 2004 Olympics.

◆ Read the conclusion below. What clues from the article support this conclusion? Write **two** clues and their paragraph numbers. Then explain how what you already know supports this conclusion.

2. **Conclusion:** Gardner's training and experience as a wrestler helped him survive his snowmobile incident in Cottonwood Canyon.

Clue/Paragraph: _____

Clue/Paragraph: _____

What I Know: _____

_____ Number of Correct Answers: Part B

C Using Words

◆ Cross out one of the four words in each row that does not relate to the word in dark type.

1. precludes

disqualify   stop   impossible   eager

2. hypothermia

light   medical   warmth   condition

3. oblivion

disconnected   lost   angry   unaware

4. minute

microscopic   realize   magnify   enormous

5. acquitting

performing   manners   entrance   deeds

◆ Choose one of the words shown in dark type above. Write a sentence using the word.

6. word: _____

_____

_____

_____ Number of Correct Answers: Part C

 **Writing About It**

Write a Story

◆ Write a story about what happened to Rulon Gardner after his snowmobile accident in 2002. Include details about how he came back to wrestle in the Olympics. Write **at least four** sentences. Use the checklist on page 103 to check your work.

_____

_____

_____

_____

_____

_____

_____

_____

Lesson 6 Add your correct answers from parts A, B, and C to get your total score. Then find the percentage for your total score on the chart below. Record your percentage on the graph on page 105.

_____ Total Score for Parts A, B, and C

_____ Percentage

Total Score	1	2	3	4	5	6	7	8	9	10	11	12	13
Percentage	8	15	23	31	38	46	54	62	69	77	85	92	100

Compare and Contrast

◆ Think about the celebrities in Unit Two. Pick two articles that tell about celebrities who had to address a problem or weakness that they had. Use information from the articles to fill in this chart.

Celebrity's Name		
What problem or weakness did the celebrity have to address?		
How did the celebrity address it?		
What happened as a result?		

Queen Latifah

Savion Glover

Tiger Woods

Queen Latifah

Feminine and Strong

Birth Name Dana Elaine Owens

Birth Date and Place March 18, 1970; Newark, New Jersey

Home Newark, New Jersey

Think About What You Know

Do you feel that you are a confident person? What gives you self-confidence? Read the article to find out about Queen Latifah and her strong sense of self.

Word Power

What do the words below tell you about the article?

immune not affected by or not vulnerable to something

apartheid an official policy of separating people based on their race

gamut the entire range or extent of something

pigeonholed put into one limited category

apathy a lack of interest, concern, or desire to act

Reading Skill

Asking Questions to Get Information Good readers **ask questions.** Asking and answering questions as you read can help you find the most important ideas in the text. Make sure to ask questions about the big ideas. Asking questions that start with *what, where, when, how,* and *why* can help you find the big ideas.

Example

There are many reasons why people choose to change their names. People often change their last names when they get married. Some choose to change their names to honor or reclaim a part of family history. Others may feel that their birth name just doesn't suit their personality.

"*Why* do people change their names?" is one question you might ask yourself to help you find important information in this paragraph. Why do you think this is such a good question to ask about this paragraph?

Queen Latifah

Feminine and Strong

Anyone who thought the world of rap music was going to be dominated exclusively by men apparently hadn't expected Queen Latifah to come along. And anyone who thought Queen Latifah's rapping would be her only claim to fame was seriously underestimating her. Over the last 15 years this tough, talented woman has risen from the streets of East Newark, New Jersey, to become a fiercely independent and hugely successful rap singer, producer, actress, talk show host, and writer.

2   Queen Latifah was born Dana Elaine Owens on March 18, 1970, in Newark, New Jersey to a schoolteacher mother and a police-officer father. After her parents divorced in 1978, Latifah moved into a public housing project in East Newark with her mother and brother.

3   They lived in a dangerous neighborhood, one that taught Latifah plenty about life in seedy nightclubs and dimly lit back alleys. "My brother kind of stayed home, but I would wander out," she says, noting, "I had a compulsive need to find out new things . . . I had to discover the world." She witnessed everything from robberies to nightclub brawls, and admits that she made some bad decisions—adding that even today she is not **immune** to bad judgment. "I make a lot of mistakes," she acknowledges.

4   Latifah quickly developed a tough, street-smart exterior, but inside she remained a young woman with a strong sense of self-worth and a refusal to be limited by the opinions of others. As proof, just consider the name "Latifah," which she adopted at age eight when a cousin raised in the Muslim faith told her the name suited her because it means "delicate and sensitive" in Arabic. "That's me," she declares, saying, "I was big for my age, and I played sports, but inside I felt I was delicate." She had always considered the name "Dana" a

bit tomboyish, so she readily took on this new name, later adding "Queen" because it sounded not only feminine but powerful as well.

5   In high school, Latifah began rapping with two of her friends, Tangy B and Landy D. Known initially as Ladies Fresh and later as Flavor Unit, they would often journey into New York City to hone their skills by performing in nightclubs. There Latifah caught the attention of a record producer, who ultimately signed her to a recording contract with Tommy Boy Records.

6   Her first single, "Wrath of My Madness," came out in 1988, and her first album, *All Hail the Queen,* was released a year later. The album combined hip-hop, reggae, and jazz with powerful lyrics about **apartheid,** poverty, and civil rights. The album's positive imagery, proud feminism, and fresh sound helped make it a tremendous hit, selling over a million copies.

7   Latifah's rise to fame is not a simple success story, however, for there has also been great sadness in her life. In 1992 her brother died in an accident while riding a motorcycle she had given him for his birthday. Latifah was devastated. "I would cry, but then I'd just go completely numb," she says. To this day she wears the key to that motorcycle around her neck as one way of remembering her brother. She also honored his memory by creating a college scholarship foundation in his name and by dedicating her album *Black Reign* to him.

Skill Break

Asking Questions to Get Information

Look at paragraph 5 on this page. The paragraph describes Queen Latifah's early experiences as a rapper.

What would be a good **question** to ask to find the **important information** in this paragraph?

What is the **answer** to your question?

8   After securing her success as a rapper with the Grammy award-winning song "U.N.I.T.Y." and releasing another hit album called *Order in the Court,* Latifah went on to establish her own recording management firm, which she called Flavor Unit Management. She also began an acting career. From 1993 to 1998, she starred in the TV sitcom *Living Single,* and in 1999 she hosted her own television talk show, *The Queen Latifah Show.* She made guest appearances on such popular series as *Ellen, Spin City,* and *Fresh Prince of Bel Air,* and she appeared in more than a dozen movies, with her roles running the **gamut** from bank robber in *Set It Off* (1996) to jazz singer in *Living Out Loud* (1998). Her biggest triumph on film came in 2002 when she played a sassy prison warden named Mama Morton in the musical hit *Chicago.* Latifah was so effective in this role that she received an Academy Award nomination for Best Supporting Actress.

9   The following year, Latifah teamed up with comedian Steve Martin to make the movie *Bringing Down the House,* a comedy with serious underlying themes. Latifah, who plays a prison inmate posing as a lawyer, explains that the movie contains "parts that challenge racial ideas and issues." The movie, she declares, "paints a picture of how ignorant racism is, how ignorant stereotypes are, but through humor."

10   In 2005 Latifah starred in *Beauty Shop,* this time playing a single mother with a daughter who is a musical genius. Not wanting to be **pigeonholed** as just a singer, Latifah was attracted to the role because it didn't require her to sing. She explains, ". . . with the scripts I've been getting, any excuse will do to have me sing in a movie, and that's not how I like to use the gift."

Fun Facts

▸ Latifah played power forward on her high school basketball team, helping the team win two state championships.

▸ When asked if she would like to be as slim as a fashion model, she says, "I like myself the way I am."

Queen Latifah performs as part of the Sugar Water Festival, a music festival she created in partnership with fellow musical artists Erykah Badu and Jill Scott.

11   Despite her many successes, Latifah has not adopted a flashy Hollywood attitude. As she laughingly reports, her mother will not let her. "Well, I go home and visit my mom, and she makes me take out the garbage and walk the dog," chuckles Latifah, "and that pretty much takes away from the Queen Latifah-ism." As Latifah says, even an Academy Award nomination means nothing "when momma makes you walk the dog."

12   In 1999 Latifah wrote an autobiographical book titled *Ladies First: Revelations of a Strong Woman.* In it, she writes, "I am not a psychologist or a sociologist. I don't have any degrees, and I'm not an expert on life. What I am is a young black woman from the inner city who is making it, despite the odds, despite the obstacles I've had to face in the lifetimes that have come my way."

13   Latifah hopes more young people in the inner city will do the same thing. She would like to see them shake off their **apathy,** stand up for their rights, and take responsibility for their own destiny. Regarding her decision to call herself "Queen Latifah," she declares that she would like to "let every woman know that she, too . . . is royalty."

A   Understanding What You Read

◆ Fill in the circle next to the correct answer.

1. Choose the statement below that states a fact.

○ A. The name "Dana" was too tomboyish.

○ B. Her album had a wonderfully fresh sound.

○ C. She was nominated for an Academy Award.

2. Latifah admits that she made mistakes

○ A. on her first rap album.

○ B. in her selection of movie roles.

○ C. growing up in East Newark.

3. Latifah honored her brother by

○ A. creating a college scholarship foundation.

○ B. wearing his initials around her neck.

○ C. buying him a new album.

4. From what you read in the article, which of these is probably true?

○ A. Latifah is afraid of dogs.

○ B. Latifah has a close relationship with her family.

○ C. Latifah has a vacation home in South Africa.

5. Which sentence **best** states the lesson about life that this article teaches?

○ A. We have to appreciate the good times while they last.

○ B. You can take responsibility for your own destiny.

○ C. Listening to others is more important than speaking.

_____ Number of Correct Answers: Part A

B Asking Questions to Get Information

◆ Read the paragraph below. Fill in the circle next to the **best** question to ask to find important information in the paragraph.

1.

The following year, Latifah teamed up with comedian Steve Martin to make the movie *Bringing Down the House,* a comedy with serious underlying themes. Latifah, who plays a prison inmate posing as a lawyer, explains that the movie contains "parts that challenge racial ideas and issues." The movie, she declares, "paints a picture of how ignorant racism is, how ignorant stereotypes are, but through humor."

○ A. How did Queen Latifah and comedian Steve Martin meet?
○ B. What lesson is taught in the movie *Bringing Down the House?*
○ C. Who else starred in the movie *Bringing Down the House?*

◆ Reread paragraph 13 in the article. Write **one** question that would help you find the most important information in the paragraph. Then write the answer to your question.

2. Question: _____

_____

Answer: _____

_____

_____ Number of Correct Answers: Part B

C Using Words

◆ The words and phrases in the list below relate to the words in the box. Some words or phrases in the list have the same meaning or a similar meaning as a word in the box. Some have the opposite meaning. Write the related word from the box on each line. Use each word from the box twice.

immune	**gamut**	**apathy**
apartheid	**pigeonholed**	

Same or similar meaning

1. categorized _____

2. not caring _____

3. protected _____

4. limited _____

5. divisions between people _____

6. the full range _____

Opposite meaning

7. only one part _____

8. unable to resist _____

9. community integration _____

10. enthusiasm _____

_____ Number of Correct Answers: Part C

D Writing About It

Write a Comic Strip

◆ Write a comic strip about Queen Latifah and her mom. Look at what's happening in each scene. Then write **at least two** sentences in each bubble. Use the checklist on page 103 to check your work.

Lesson 7 Add your correct answers from parts A, B, and C to get your total score. Then find the percentage for your total score on the chart below. Record your percentage on the graph on page 105.

_____ Total Score for Parts A, B, and C

_____ Percentage

Total Score	1	2	3	4	5	6	7	8	9	10	11	12	13	14	15	16	17
Percentage	6	12	18	24	29	35	41	47	53	59	65	70	76	82	88	94	100

Savion Glover

Tap-Dancing Genius

Birth Name Savion Glover

Birthdate and Place November 19, 1973; Newark, New Jersey

Home New York City, New York

Think About What You Know

Are you aware of the rhythms in the world around you, such as footsteps on stairs or raindrops on the roof? Read the article and find out how Savion Glover uses his natural sense of rhythm to create his unique style of dancing.

Word Power

What do the words below tell you about the article?

passé out of date or no longer in style

unorthodox unusual or different from what is commonly accepted

alienated having a feeling of not belonging

vignettes short performances that tell a story

collaborated worked in cooperation with others

Reading Skill

Fact and Opinion A **fact** is a statement that can be proved by checking a research source. If a statement cannot be proved, it is an opinion. An **opinion** is someone's own idea or belief about something. When a statement includes words that show judgment, such as *best, should, excellent,* or *beautiful,* that statement usually contains someone's opinion.

Example	
Fact	Percussive dance is a term used to describe all dance forms that emphasize the sounds produced by the dancers.
Opinion	Tap dancing is the most beautiful and exciting form of percussive dance.

The first sentence in the paragraph states a fact. The definition of "percussive dance" can be checked in a dictionary or encyclopedia and proved to be correct. The second sentence in the paragraph is an opinion. It shows a judgment about the relationship between tap dancing and other forms of percussive dance. What words or phrases in the second statement show that the statement expresses an opinion?

Savion Glover

Tap-Dancing Genius

Before Savion Glover, many people thought tap dancing was **passé** a "corny, washed-up art form" occasionally featured in grainy old black-and-white movies but otherwise abandoned by everyone except a few tuxedoed gentlemen who tapped out only precisely choreographed steps. For Glover, though, tap dancing is something entirely different: it is a vibrant experience filled with urgent rhythms and unpredictable moves. "It's new and it's raw," he says; it's "like air—it's alive." Tap dancing is Glover's career—and his passion.

2   Glover grew up in Newark, New Jersey, where he lived with his mother, two older brothers, his grandmother, his aunt, and her nephew. "The house was crazy," he recalls, and it couldn't have helped that even as a toddler Glover added to the chaos by constantly banging on pots and pans or grabbing his fork and knife and tapping them against the walls. His early explorations of rhythm didn't go unnoticed; when he was three years old, his mother, Yvette, signed him up for percussion classes.

3   Glover hadn't been drumming long when the instructor took Yvette aside and told her that Glover "had to go." Although Yvette initially assumed her son had violated some rule and was being expelled from the class for disciplinary reasons, that was not the case. The teacher said Glover showed so much talent that he should go audition at the Newark Community School of the Arts. He did, and by age five had been awarded a full scholarship to attend the school. Two years after that, Yvette enrolled him in a tap-dancing class at the Broadway Dance Center in Manhattan. Unable to afford real tap-dancing shoes, she sent him off to class wearing beat-up old cowboy boots, which sufficed until he finally got real tap shoes seven months later.

4   Even with his **unorthodox** footwear, Glover loved tap dancing class and was soon tapping out a beat wherever he went: in stores, on city sidewalks, and even barefoot in the shower. Tap dancing provided the perfect vehicle for expressing rhythms, ideas, and emotions. He experimented with the different sounds his feet could make, eventually becoming master of a style called "rhythm tap," which uses every part of the foot, not just the heel and toe, to produce different noises. By hitting the floor with his baby toe, his big toe, or the side of his foot, Glover creates subtle variations in tone, thus expanding the range of sounds that his feet can produce.

5   It isn't just the sounds he creates that sets Glover apart from other tap dancers, it's his approach to dancing. He has what he describes as a "rough, funky, underground" style that requires furious foot movement and intense amounts of energy. Glover virtually attacks the wooden floor, pounding out a wide array of rhythms with amazing exuberance. Dressed in baggy pants, with dreadlocks bouncing and sweat flying off his body, he projects a distinctly different look from the ballroom elegance of Fred Astaire or the happy-go-lucky image of Bill "Bojangles" Robinson, two great tap dancers of the past. In fact, much of the time Glover is so focused on his feet that he turns his back to his audience and hunches forward in intense concentration.

6   It didn't take long for Glover's talent to gain him a wide audience. When he was just 10 years old he was recruited for a Broadway show called *Tap Dance Kid,* and by the time he was seventeen he had performed in Europe, starred in the movie *Tap,* and had been hired as a cast member on the children's show *Sesame Street.*

Skill Break

Fact and Opinion

Look at paragraph 3 on page 78. The paragraph describes Glover's first experiences taking percussion and tap dancing classes.

Which sentence in this paragraph shows someone's **opinion?**

Why is this an opinion?

7   "I like to do positive things," Glover says in reference to his time on *Sesame Street,* "to be thought of as a positive model, someone kids can relate to." Besides, he points out, *Sesame Street* was lots of fun, and fun is something Glover values highly. He recognizes that many African American youths feel **alienated** from the mainstream culture, and he considers himself fortunate to have found a niche with his tap dancing. "If I didn't have the dance to express myself," he says, "I would probably be stealing your car or selling drugs right now . . . Tap saved me."

8   Glover's biggest break came in 1996 when he teamed up with producer George Wolfe to create the Broadway blockbuster *Bring in 'Da Noise, Bring in 'Da Funk.* This musical, which Glover choreographed and starred in, features a series of tap-dancing **vignettes** that tell the history of African Americans in the United States from the time of slavery to the present day. It was fitting for Glover to create a tap-dancing show about this topic, since tap has deep roots in the African American community. As Glover can tell you, tap dancing developed on the streets of New York City in the nineteenth century when African dance steps were blended with various European moves.

9   *Bring in 'Da Noise* was a huge success, and at age 22, Glover found himself the recipient of a Tony Award for Best Choreographer. He followed this up with another appearance in the movies, this time in Spike Lee's film *Bamboozled.* Glover also put together a special dance performance as a tribute to the great jazz artist John Coltrane;

Fun Facts

▶ As a child, Glover studied jazz dancing and ballet as well as tap.

▶ He wears size 12½ EE (extra wide) shoes.

▶ Tap dancing is such intense, sweaty work that Glover typically changes shirts three times during a performance.

Savion Glover demonstrates his unique tap-dancing style while performing at a jazz festival in Hollywood.

for another show he **collaborated** with four musicians in a string quartet and tapped to classical music. Glover takes pride in the fluid nature of his performances, saying, "Most of what I do comes to me while I'm on stage. When we're rehearsing a show I'm thinking about the steps and the lighting and all of it, but once we start, most of it happens up there."

10   Glover's talent is nothing short of amazing. Although people have called him a "genius," a "miracle," and a "savior of tap," Glover himself is full of humility, saying, "I'm just a tap dancer, man." He credits a long line of dancers who preceded him, saying they paved the way for his success. At the top of that list is the late Gregory Hines, the man who—until Glover came along—was considered the best tap dancer of modern times. In fact, Glover has called Hines "my father, best friend, brother, guru, mentor."

11   Given the explosion of interest in tap dancing that Glover's work has created, it seems safe to predict that tap dancing, or "hoofing" as it is often called, will be around for a long time to come. Certainly Glover can't imagine a life without it; tap dancing is all about rhythm, and as Glover says, "rhythm is everywhere."

Understanding What You Read

◆ Fill in the circle next to the correct answer or write the answer.

1. Before he began tap-dancing classes, Glover took classes to learn how to

   ○ A. act.
   ○ B. drum.
   ○ C. cook.

2. In which paragraph did you find your information to answer question 1?

   _____

3. When Glover dances he uses every part of his foot in order to

   ○ A. give his dancing more energy.
   ○ B. create more variations in sound.
   ○ C. help him move his feet faster.

4. If you were a dance teacher, how could you use the information in the article to help you teach your students?

   ○ A. I would teach dance classes in rhythm-tap style only.
   ○ B. I would have my tap-dancing students wear cowboy boots.
   ○ C. I would encourage students to be creative and try new steps.

5. Choose from the letters below to correctly complete the following statement. Write the letters on the lines.

   In the article, _____ and _____ are similar.

   A. Savion Glover's dancing style
   B. Fred Astaire's dancing style
   C. rhythm-tap dancing

   _____ Number of Correct Answers: Part A

B Understanding Fact and Opinion

◆ Read the paragraph below. Write the letter *O* on the lines next to the statements that show someone's opinion. Write the letter *F* on the lines next to the statements that are facts.

1.

Before Savion Glover, many people thought tap dancing was passé, a "corny, washed-up art form" occasionally featured in grainy old black-and-white movies but otherwise abandoned by everyone except a few tuxedoed gentlemen who tapped out only precisely choreographed steps. For Glover, though, tap dancing is something entirely different: it is a vibrant experience filled with urgent rhythms and unpredictable moves. "It's new and it's raw," he says; it's "like air—it's alive." Tap dancing is Glover's career—and his passion.

_____ Tap dancing is a vibrant experience filled with urgent rhythms.

_____ Tap dancing is like air.

_____ Tap dancing is Glover's career.

◆ Reread paragraph 10 in the article. Write **one** statement from the paragraph that shows an opinion. Then explain why it is an opinion statement.

2. Opinion: _____

_____

Why is this an opinion? _____

_____

_____ Number of Correct Answers: Part B

C Using Words

◆ Complete the analogies below by writing a word from the box on each line. Remember that in an analogy, the last two words or phrases must be related in the same way that the first two are related.

passé	alienated	collaborated
unorthodox	vignettes	

1. sea : ocean :: dramatic scenes : _____

2. simple : complicated :: welcome : _____

3. laughing : crying :: new : _____

4. seeing : viewing :: shared : _____

5. calm : excited :: regular : _____

◆ Choose one word from the box. Write a sentence using the word.

6. word: _____

_____

_____

_____ Number of Correct Answers: Part C

D Writing About It

Describe a Person

◆ Write a description of Savion Glover during one of his tap-dancing performances. Describe his dance style and the way he looks and sounds. Write **at least four** sentences. Use the checklist on page 103 to check your work.

_____

_____

_____

_____

_____

_____

_____

_____

Lesson 8 Add your correct answers from parts A, B, and C to get your total score. Then find the percentage for your total score on the chart below. Record your percentage on the graph on page 105.

_____ Total Score for Parts A, B, and C

_____ Percentage

Total Score	1	2	3	4	5	6	7	8	9	10	11	12	13
Percentage	8	15	23	31	38	46	54	62	69	77	85	92	100

Tiger Woods

Master of the Fairways

Birth Name Eldrick T. Woods

Birth Date and Place December 30, 1975; Cypress, California

Home Orlando, Florida

Think About What You Know

Have you ever played golf or watched a golf tournament? Does it seem like a difficult sport to learn? Read the article and find out how Tiger Woods made his ascent to the highest levels of professional golf.

Word Power

What do the words below tell you about the article?

proclivities natural attractions toward something

pedigrees lines of ancestry, especially ones that are highly respected

rigor mortis the stiffening of the muscles in the body that begins shortly after death

relinquished gave up or let go of

preeminent outstanding

Reading Skill

Drawing Conclusions Good readers **draw conclusions.** They combine information from several parts of an article with what they already know to find a bigger idea. As you read, look for details in the text that provide clues about the people and events in the article. Evaluate the clues carefully. Your conclusions should be supported by at least two clues in the text.

Example

A golf ball has been made that goes 25 yards farther than regular golf balls when hit with the same force. This new golf-ball technology allows hard-hitting golfers to complete today's most challenging professional golf courses with ease. Courses that were once considered difficult are no longer a match for many professional golfers.

What do you already know about technology? One thing you might know is that *new technology can help athletes perform better.* So a conclusion that you might draw from this paragraph is that *people who build new golf courses will need to make them more challenging.* What are two clues from the paragraph that support this conclusion?

Tiger Woods

Master of the Fairways

Many people want to get their children off to an early start in sports, but Earl Woods took that concept to its extreme. Determined to mold his son, Tiger, into a star golfer, Earl Woods encouraged the boy to start swinging a club when he was just 9 months old. At the age of 18 months, Tiger played his first hole, toddling along the fairway to complete a 410-yard hole in just 11 strokes. And at age 3, Tiger could finish a 9-hole course in just 48 strokes. Many amateur adult golfers strive to shoot a score that low.

2   Woods was such a remarkable golfer so early in his life that it was impossible for people not to be impressed. Indeed, he caught the eye of many observers, appearing on TV on the *Mike Douglas Show* when he was two years old and gracing the pages of *Golf Digest* magazine at age five.

3   Children who are thrust into a sport at such a tender age frequently burn out by the time they are teenagers, but in Woods's case his passion—and talent—for golf seemed to expand with each passing year. By the time he was 13 he was an expert at producing backspin on the ball and could hit a practice drive over a 50-foot-high barrier that was 225 yards away. Of course no golfer is perfect, and Woods's game still needed some refinement; although he could hit the ball a tremendous distance, his shots tended to be wild and his game somewhat unpredictable. As Earl Woods laughingly recalled, "I used to tell him he was aptly named because he was always in the woods."

4   As for Tiger's first name, Earl Woods had come up with the name "Tiger" not because of his son's golfing **proclivities** but as a way to honor an old friend. Earl, who served as a lieutenant colonel in the U.S. Army during the Vietnam War, had struck up a friendship with a Vietnamese soldier named Vuong Dang Phong, a man so tough and fearless in combat that Earl had called him "Tiger."

5   Earl later lost touch with Phong but vowed that if he ever had a baby, he would give that baby Phong's nickname. So although Earl and his wife, Kultida, named their only child Eldrick, Earl kept his vow and nicknamed the boy "Tiger." Earl declared, "If it had been a girl, she would have been Tiger, too."

6   Tiger's name is not his sole connection to Asia; both his parents have some Asian ancestors. His mother is half Thai, one-quarter Chinese, and one-quarter white, whereas his father was half African American, one-quarter Native American, and one-quarter Chinese. Although such mixed ancestry is increasingly common, Tiger Woods is the first professional golfer to bring such a rich racial and ethnic background to the game. Before he came along, golf was predominantly a country-club sport played by wealthy white men with European **pedigrees.** Now, thanks in large measure to Woods, there is an explosion of interest in golf among young people of all races and nationalities.

7   The young Woods continued to hone his golf skills, and at age 16 he won his first U.S. Junior Amateur Championship, a tournament he won the following two years as well. When he was 16 he also secured an exemption to compete in the Los Angeles Open. At that time this made him the youngest golfer ever to play in a regular Professional Golf Association (PGA) Tour event. Understandably nervous to be playing against seasoned professionals, Woods, who was merely a high school sophomore at the time, did not excel in this tournament.

Skill Break
Drawing Conclusions

Look at paragraph 6 on this page. The paragraph describes the significance of Tiger Woods's ethnic background. One conclusion a reader might draw from this paragraph is that *Tiger Woods may have faced racial discrimination when he began golfing.*

Can you find at least **two clues** that support this conclusion?

How does **what you already know** support this conclusion?

"I was so tense I had a tough time holding the club," he later admitted, adding, "it was like **rigor mortis** had set in." Although he didn't ever threaten the leaders, he did manage to beat 15 of the pros who were playing that day, including Andy North, a two-time U.S. Open Champion.

8   When Woods turned 18, he graduated from the ranks of junior amateurs and entered the U.S. Amateur Championship, where he competed against the most accomplished amateurs of all ages. Woods won this competition three years in a row, becoming the first golfer ever to do so.

9   Finally, at the age of 20, Woods **relinquished** his amateur status and turned professional. He signed a $40 million, five-year endorsement contract with a major sportswear company on August 29, 1996, and the next day made his professional debut, playing in the Greater Milwaukee Open. On that day thousands of spectators clustered around the fairway to witness Woods's first shot. He didn't disappoint them, hitting a 336-yard drive straight down the middle. Woods shot seven under par for the tournament, even achieving the ultimate rarity, a hole-in-one, during the final round. Others had better scores, though, and Woods finished tied for 60th place, garnering a $2,544 paycheck.

10   Over the next few months, Woods worked on elevating his game and learning to cope with the immense following of fans who materialized wherever he played. Luckily his quiet demeanor and calm personality helped him handle the stress of his celebrity status. As he puts it, "I'm not a person who ranges in emotion from high to low; I've always been more or less pretty mellow."

Fun Facts

- Woods was eight years old when he sank his first hole-in-one.
- In 1975 Lee Elder was the first African American golfer to play in the Masters.
- Woods says of Elder and other early African American golfers, "He was the one I looked up to . . . I was able to live my dream because of those guys."

Tiger Woods attempts a difficult shot during the final round of the 2005 Masters in Augusta, Georgia.

11   Woods revealed his ability to handle pressure during the 1997 Masters in Augusta, Georgia. While there are an abundance of tournaments on the PGA tour, the Masters is one of only four events that are considered "majors," the three others being the U.S. Open, the British Open, and the PGA Championship. Woods began the '97 Masters poorly, going four over par for his first nine holes. Then he settled in and made a spectacular comeback, surpassing his opponents with unprecedented ease and surging to a commanding lead. When he sank his final putt and walked off the 18th green, he walked into the history books by finishing 18 under par, the lowest score ever recorded at the Masters. In addition, he was the youngest golfer to win the Masters, and the first non-white player to wear the green jacket, the traditional garment bestowed upon the winner.

12   Since then Woods has been the dominant force in professional golf. He has already won all four majors, some more than once. People expected great things from Tiger Woods since the beginning. He not only met these expectations but exceeded them to become the **preeminent** golfer of his time.

A Understanding What You Read

◆ Fill in the circle next to the correct answer.

1. When he was 13 years old, Woods needed to refine his game because
   ○ A. his swing was not strong enough.
   ○ B. his shots tended to be wild.
   ○ C. he didn't get enough spin on the ball.

2. How is Tiger Woods an example of a genius?
   ○ A. At age 3 he finished a 9-hole course in 48 strokes.
   ○ B. He was the first non-white player to win the Masters.
   ○ C. At the Greater Milwaukee Open he played very well.

3. Woods was nicknamed "Tiger" because of
   ○ A. his tough and fearless golf game.
   ○ B. the love his mother has for Asian animals.
   ○ C. a man that his father knew in Vietnam.

4. From the information in the article, you can predict that
   ○ A. there will be a large increase in the number of pro golfers.
   ○ B. many parents will start to teach their babies to play golf.
   ○ C. there will be more pro golfers who are people of color.

5. Which sentence **best** states the main idea of the article?
   ○ A. Woods started young and became the top golfer of his time.
   ○ B. Woods has a diverse cultural background.
   ○ C. Woods made sports history with his record-breaking wins.

_____ Number of Correct Answers: Part A

Drawing Conclusions

◆ Read the conclusion below. Write the letter C on the line next to each clue that supports this conclusion.

1. Conclusion: Once Earl Woods made a decision about something, he was not likely to change his mind.

_____ Earl was determined to mold his son into a star golfer.

_____ Earl served as a lieutenant colonel in the U.S. Army during the Vietnam War.

_____ Earl vowed that if he had a child he would nickname the child "Tiger."

_____ Earl was part African American, Native American, and Chinese.

_____ Earl said, "If it had been a girl, she would have been Tiger, too."

◆ Read the conclusion below. What clues from the article support this conclusion? Write **two** clues and their paragraph numbers. Then explain how what you already know supports this conclusion.

2. Conclusion: Tiger Woods did things as a child and as a teenager that most adults only dream of doing.

Clue/Paragraph: _____

Clue/Paragraph: _____

What I Know: _____

_____ Number of Correct Answers: Part B

93

C Using Words

◆ Cross out one of the four words in each row that does not relate to the word in dark type.

1. proclivities

    likings   abilities   desires   certificates

2. pedigrees

    manager   ancestor   lineage   royal

3. rigor mortis

    movement   tissue   separate   inflexible

4. relinquished

    discard   panic   quit   surrender

5. preeminent

    connect   amaze   supreme   exceed

◆ Choose one of the words shown in dark type above. Write a sentence using the word.

6. word: _____

_____

_____

⬚ _____ Number of Correct Answers: Part C

94

D Writing About It

Write a Journal Entry

◆ Suppose you were a spectator at the Greater Milwaukee Open the year Tiger Woods made his professional debut. Write a journal entry describing what you might have seen that day. Write **at least four** sentences. Use the chart on page 103 to check your work.

_____

_____

_____

_____

_____

_____

_____

_____

Lesson 9 Add your correct answers from parts A, B, and C to get your total score. Then find the percentage for your total score on the chart below. Record your percentage on the graph on page 105.

_____ Total Score for Parts A, B, and C

_____ Percentage

Total Score	1	2	3	4	5	6	7	8	9	10	11	12	13
Percentage	8	15	23	31	38	46	54	62	69	77	85	92	100

Compare and Contrast

◆ Think about the celebrities in Unit Three. Pick two articles that tell about celebrities who disproved a widely held belief. Use information from the articles to fill in this chart.

Celebrity's Name		
What belief did the celebrity disprove?		
How did the celebrity disprove the belief?		
What happened as a result?		

Glossary

A

accessibility   openness or approachability   p. 48

accolades   praise, awards, or honors   p. 17

acquitting   behaving in a certain way   p. 59

adulation   exaggerated praise or flattery   p. 39

alienated   having a feeling of not belonging   p. 80

apartheid   an official policy of separating people based on their race   p. 69

apathy   a lack of interest, concern, or desire to act   p. 71

B

banter   good-natured, witty conversation   p. 14

C

cajoling   gently persuading someone with soothing talk and promises   p. 24

collaborated   worked in cooperation with others   p. 81

compiling   collecting or putting together   p. 25

D

demoted   reduced to a lower rank   p. 47

E

echelon   a particular level of authority or responsibility   p. 39

effusive   showing excessive feelings   p. 14

endorsing   giving support or approval to   p. 7

G

gamut   the entire range or extent of something   p. 70

H

hypothermia   a condition of dangerously low body temperature caused by being in the cold too long   p. 57

I

illiterates   people who are unable to read or write   p. 5

immune   not affected by or not vulnerable to something   p. 68

impoverished   very poor   p. 46

insatiable   not able to be satisfied   p. 4

instilled   introduced or taught something over a period of time   p. 46

insufferable   unbearable or not to be tolerated   p. 14

integral   necessary to the completeness of the whole   p. 37

integrity   honesty or moral decency   p. 17

M

maraca   a rattle-like musical instrument made from a hollow gourd containing seeds or pebbles   p. 39

memorabilia   objects valued for their connection with a particular person, event, or interest   p. 38

minute   very small   p. 59

O

oblivion   a state of unconsciousness   p. 57

P

passé   out of date or no longer in style   p. 78

pedigrees   lines of ancestry, especially ones that are highly respected   p. 89

perfectionist   someone who sets extremely high personal standards   p. 4

pigeonholed   put into one limited category   p. 70

pivotal   of central importance   p. 26

precludes   prevents someone from doing something   p. 56

preeminent   outstanding   p. 91

proclivities   natural attractions toward something   p. 88

R

reconvened   met or came together again   p. 26

relinquished   gave up or let go of   p. 90

rigor mortis   the stiffening of the muscles in the body that begins shortly after death   p. 90

S

sharecropper   a farmer who farms on someone else's land in return for a share of the crops   p. 4

syndication   a system of selling a television show to many different stations   p. 47

T

tenacity   a state of not giving up when trying to reach a goal or desired outcome   p. 24

U

unorthodox   unusual or different from what is commonly accepted   p. 79

V

vignettes   short performances that tell a story   p. 80

My Personal Dictionary

My Personal Dictionary

Writing Checklist

1. I followed the directions for writing.

2. My writing shows that I read and understood the article.

3. I started each sentence with a capital letter.

4. I put a punctuation mark at the end of each sentence.

5. My sentences all have a subject and a verb.

6. I capitalized proper nouns.

7. I read my writing aloud and listened for missing words.

8. I used a dictionary to check words that don't look right.

◆ Use the chart below to check off the things on the list that you have done.

✓ Checklist Numbers	Lesson Numbers								
	1	2	3	4	5	6	7	8	9
1.									
2.									
3.									
4.									
5.									
6.									
7.									
8.									

Progress Check

You can take charge of your own progress. The Comprehension and Critical Thinking Progress Graph on the next page can help you. Use it to keep track of how you are doing as you work through the lessons in this book. Check the graph often with your teacher. What types of skills cause you trouble? Talk with your teacher about ways to work on these.

A sample Comprehension and Critical Thinking Progress Graph is shown below. The first three lessons have been filled in to show you how to use the graph.

Sample Comprehension and Critical Thinking Progress Graph

◆ **Directions:** Write your percentage score for each lesson in the box under the number of the lesson. Then put a small X on the line. The X goes above the number of the lesson and across from the score you earned. Chart your progress by drawing a line to connect the Xs.

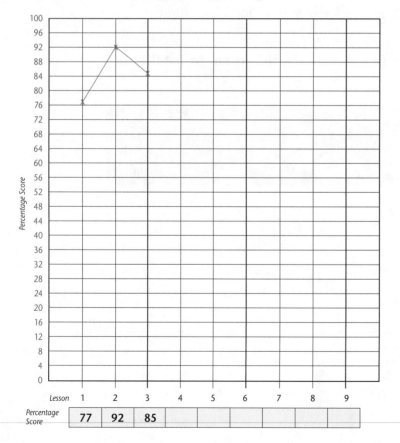

Lesson	1	2	3	4	5	6	7	8	9
Percentage Score	77	92	85						

Comprehension and Critical Thinking Progress Graph

◆ **Directions:** Write your percentage score for each lesson in the box under the number of the lesson. Then put a small X on the line. The X goes above the number of the lesson and across from the score you earned. Chart your progress by drawing a line to connect the Xs.

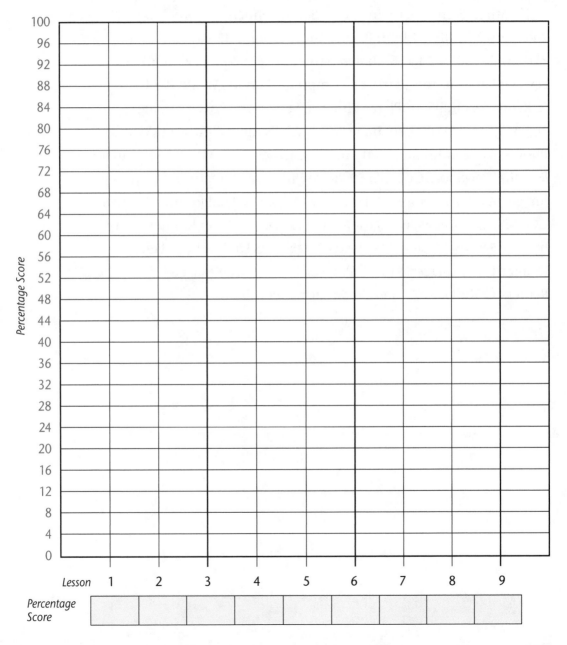

Photo Credits

Cover Ronald Martinez/Getty Images, (inset)Don Emmert/AFP/Getty Images; 1 (t)Reuters/CORBIS, (c)Vaughn Youtz/ZUMA/CORBIS, (b)Jonathan Ferrey/Getty Images; 2 Sarah Lehberger/Getty Images; 7 Reuters/CORBIS; 12 John Rogers/Getty Images; 17 Vaughn Youtz/ZUMA/CORBIS; 22 Ray Stubblebine/Reuters/CORBIS; 27 Jonathan Ferrey/Getty Images; 33 (t)Jack Dempsey/AP/Wide World Photos, (c)Reuters/CORBIS, (b)Pierre-Philippe Marcou/AFP/Getty Images; 34 Jeff Haynes/AFP/Getty Images; 39 Jack Dempsey/AP/Wide World Photos; 44 Peter Kramer/Getty Images; 49 Reuters/CORBIS; 54 William R. Salliz/NewSport/CORBIS; 59 Pierre-Philippe Marcou/AFP/Getty Images; 65 (t)Tim Mosenfelder/Getty Images, (c)Fred Prouser/Reuters/CORBIS, (b)Andrew Redington/Getty Images; 66 Peter Kramer/Getty Images; 71 Tim Mosenfelder/Getty Images; 75 Pat Lewis; 76 Peter Kramer/Getty Images; 81 Fred Prouser/Reuters/CORBIS; 86 Jeff Mitchell/Reuters/CORBIS; 91 Andrew Redington/Getty Images.